AF541746

RBI
GOVERNORS

The Czars of Monetary Policy (1935–2021)

GOKUL RATHI

RUPA

Published by
Rupa Publications India Pvt. Ltd 2023
7/16, Ansari Road, Daryaganj
New Delhi 110002

Sales centres:
Prayagraj Bengaluru Chennai
Hyderabad Jaipur Kathmandu
Kolkata Mumbai

P-ISBN: 978-93-5702-177-7
E-ISBN: 978-93-5702-192-0

First impression 2023

10 9 8 7 6 5 4 3 2 1

Printed in India

To Dr C. Rangarajan

Contents

Foreword
by C. Rangarajan

Dr. C. Rangarajan

Former Chairman, Economic Advisory Council
to the Prime Minister
Former Governor, Reserve Bank of India

Chairman
Madras School of Economics
Gandhi Mandapam Road, Kottur
Chennai 600025

FOREWORD

October 25, 2021

The Central Bank occupies an important place in the Institutional framework of any country. The major responsibility of a central bank is to maintain stability and to promote growth. Stability and growth are interrelated. Sustained high growth is not possible in an environment of instability. But the connotations of stability and growth have been changing over time and are subject to many interpretations. Reserve Bank of India as the Central Bank of the country was set up in 1935. Thus it has had a history of 86 years, enough to provide insights into the multifarious functions of a central bank.

Governors of Reserve Bank have been men (so far) of eminence and scholarship and have therefore commanded respect from others including government. This book which Rathi has written is not an analytical work. It is more a catalogue of events that happened during the tenure of all the Governors. It provides the academic and administrative background of the governors, key decisions taken by them and the views expressed by others on their work. It is thus a compendium, carefully collected and interestingly presented. The work involved has been huge. I have a disclaimer. I cannot vouch for all the facts presented in the book. That is the author's responsibility. Some interesting anecdotes and tidbits are presented to make the presentation lively.

During the last eight decades, there have been contentious issues on which RBI and government have differed. Also there have been many analysts who have been trenchant critics of RBI policies. These are not the issues that have been dealt with in the book. The book is a broad-brush picture of the people who drove the Institution during the eight decades. It is interesting and sometimes amusing.

C. RANGARAJAN

Res: F-1, Rangavilas, 23/12 III Main Raod, Nanganallur, Chennai 600061
(Off)044-22300301 (Res)044-22243384 (Mob.)9445183385 Email: c.rangarajan@mse.ac.in

Foreword

by Nitin Gadkari

I am pleased to pen down a few words of prelude to the book *RBI Governors*, written by my friend Shri Gokul Rathi. This book gave me a pleasant realization that Mr Rathi is not only a chartered accountant but an ardent researcher and an erudite penman. This is perhaps first book on RBI governors, people who have played a pivotal role in defining economic and financial destiny of this vast nation and especially the banking sector that underwent enormous changes over the decades.

The RBI is one of the finest central banks in the world, and the governors who lorded over the affairs of the RBI since its inception have had their own impact on each phase of transition in the Indian economy. An RBI governor is a very powerful authority who leads a nation through ups and downs in the global economic affairs. Hence, his role impacts banking, governance and commoners as well. I came across many interesting facts about RBI governors through this book. Many of the commoners are curious about the man whose signature appears on the currency note. I am sure that readers would enjoy the very interesting facts in the book. The RBI, being the backbone of Indian economic and financial system, has, to its credit, an illustrious track record to keep this nation afloat during turmoil.

The governors have power and multiple responsibilities. Their work is very challenging. They have to be people oriented on the one side and shoulder a responsibility to keep system of governance satisfied on the other. Mr Rathi has penned down this marvellous book, giving glimpses of pre-Independence, post-Independence and post-liberalization eras of the affairs of the RBI, and roles played by the governors during their tenures. This book has a tremendous value not only for the students of economics and finance but for everybody who wishes to get to know the core of Indian banking system that shapes, impacts and determines our lives and overall social and economic well-being. I congratulate Mr Rathi for this endeavour and wish him all the best for all such future projects.

Nitin Gadkari
Minister for Road Transport and Highways,
Government of India

Preface

I have been closely associated with the banking sector throughout my professional life as an auditor, consultant and board member. I have observed the banking sector in India undergo tremendous changes during the last three decades. The volume and value of transactions have increased manifold, as have the number and diversity of products and services being offered by banks to their customers. In all of this, technology has played a major role.

The Reserve Bank of India (RBI) is central to these changes. It is the banker to the government, the authority for note issue, debt manager for the government, lender of the last resort for banks and the authority managing foreign exchange, and fulfills many other important functions. It is also responsible for maintaining price stability in the country. The functionary as the head of this institution is the governor who has onerous responsibilities. He controls the country's monetary, currency and credit systems. He has to ensure that the economy remains on track and remains safe from external shocks. He has to advise the government in policy-making and also implement the policies of the government. Among other things, the governor helps formulate, implement and monitor monetary policy.

Given the above, I was a little surprised to find that there was no book (to the best of my knowledge) that profiled all RBI governors. I was particularly impressed with the deft handling of the Indian economy by Dr Y.V. Reddy before the global financial crisis of 2007–08. Perhaps the seed for this book was sown at that time and, over the years, my resolve to plug this deficiency—notwithstanding my limitations of knowledge and experience in the literary field—only became stronger. It is only in the recent years that RBI governors have been in the media's limelight, with some actively courting the press to be there. However, in the years gone by, the RBI governor, although a public figure, had functioned pretty much behind the scenes. One of the aims of this book is to place before the public the contributions of these eminent men who aided in moulding the financial system of the country.

The idea is to provide pen portraits of RBI governors, bringing their professional achievements into sharper focus. Initially intended as a concise book with the aim of introducing the men who have helmed this formidable institution to the general reader, it has now become a mid-sized volume. My effort has been to cover, in a nutshell, major aspects of their tenure, the policies they pursued, their achievements and disappointments and, more importantly, the impact their actions had in shaping the economic policies of the country. While the contributions of the RBI's top management can hardly be ignored, each governor has been associated with a distinct style of working; it is the governor whose background, preferences and past experience has set the tone during each tenure. More importantly, it is the governor's equation with the government (read the Ministry of Finance) that has had a distinct impact on the working of the institution and its influence on the economy. The Prologue gives the reader a brief glimpse into the role of the RBI and the functions of the governor. I have also included some interesting facts and trivia at the end of some chapters in the book.

My debt to the four volumes of the official *History of the Reserve Bank of India*, Vols 1–4 (1970–2013) in writing this book is immense. Wherever possible, I have also consulted other books on the RBI, memoirs and autobiographies of former governors as well as relevant articles in newspapers and magazines. The footnotes illustrate the full scale of my debt. I can only hope that I have given citations wherever appropriate but would like to apologize in advance for any inadvertent slip. The sources of my information are clearly set out in the footnotes and give the interested reader an opportunity to follow up with further reading. They are, however, not essential to the enjoyment of the book.

I am aware that the book will need revision as and when the RBI publishes the next volume of its history covering the period 1997 onwards, in which many new facts may emerge. Till then, notwithstanding the many imperfections and limitations of the book and its author, I request the reader to accept this labour of love.

Prologue

THE RBI: ITS FUNCTIONS AND THE ROLE OF THE GOVERNOR

The RBI was established under the Reserve Bank of India Act, 1934 (RBI Act, 1934) on 1 April 1935 as a private shareholders' bank, but since its nationalization in 1949, it is fully owned by the Government of India. According to the preamble to the RBI Act, its basic objective is 'to regulate the issue of Bank notes and keeping of reserves with a view to securing monetary stability in India and generally, to operate the currency and credit system of the country to its advantage'. Thus, even though there is no explicit mandate for price stability or formal inflation targeting, over the years, maintaining price stability and ensuring adequate flow of credit to facilitate the growth process have emerged as the twin objectives of monetary policy in India. The balance between the twin objectives is dictated by prevailing circumstances and is articulated in monetary policy statements. Considerations of macroeconomic and financial stability are also subsumed in the articulation of policy.

The RBI is also entrusted with the management of foreign-exchange reserves, which are reflected in its balance sheet. While the RBI is essentially a monetary authority, its founding statute mandates it to be the manager of the public debt of the Government of India and the banker to the government. It is also entrusted with work relating to banking regulation and supervision by a separate enactment, namely, the Banking Regulation Act, 1949. The RBI exercised a tight regime of exchange control under Foreign Exchange Regulation Act (FERA), 1973, till 2000. With the enactment of the Foreign Exchange Management Act (FEMA), 1999, in May 2000, the objectives of foreign-exchange regulation were redefined as the facilitation of external trade and payments as well as the orderly development and functioning of the foreign-exchange market in India. It is significant that the RBI Act precludes the RBI from performing certain businesses such as trading; taking any direct interest in any commercial, industrial or other undertaking; purchasing of shares or granting loans against shares of any company; advancing money on the security of immovable property and drawing or accepting bills payable otherwise than on demand. These prohibitions are meant to protect the integrity of the institution.

As per Section 7(2) of the RBI Act, 1934, the 'general superintendence and direction of the affairs and business' of the RBI are entrusted to the Central Board of Directors. The Central Board, nominated by the government, consists of 14 eminent persons drawn from different walks of life. The secretary dealing with economic affairs in the Ministry of Finance is also a director on the Central Board. He/she can raise issues but cannot vote. Further, the governor and the deputy governors are also appointed by the government as the chairman and non-voting directors of the Board, respectively. The Central Board meets at least six times a year and at least once a quarter. It has the primary authority and responsibility to oversee the RBI but delegates specific functions to the local boards and various committees.

The RBI General Regulations, 1949, mandates a Committee of the Central Board (CCB), which is like an executive board and meets once a week. The CCB quorum demands the presence of at least one non-official director. The weekly meetings review the economy and developments in the financial markets and approve weekly accounts of the RBI (which are uploaded on the RBI website every week soon after their approval) and all other matters relating to the general conduct of the RBI's business. The governor (and in his absence, the senior-most deputy governor available) presides over these meetings.

The functions of supervision of the banking system and development financial institutions (DFIs), non-banking financial companies (NBFCs) and primary dealers are overseen by a separate Board for Financial Supervision (BFS), which has been constituted by the government through separate regulations formulated under the RBI Act. The BFS has four non-official Central Board directors as its members and meets at least once a month, functioning virtually as an executive board in matters relating to regulation and supervision. While the governor chairs the BFS, where all the deputy governors are members, one of the deputy governors is virtually its full-time vice-chairman. In addition to issue-based reviews and directions, the BFS reviews the functioning of individual banks. In certain cases, there is also a monthly monitoring of individual banks. Thus, in a sense, the supervision function is handled somewhat independently, but within the RBI.

Yet another body constituted by the government through a separate regulation is the Board for Payment and Settlement Systems (BPSS), which has two non-official Central Board directors as its members and meets at least once a quarter. It is the highest policy-making body on payment systems in the country. The BPSS is empowered to authorize and prescribe policies and set standards for regulating and supervising all the payment and settlement systems in the country. The Department of Payment and Settlement Systems of the RBI serves as the secretariat to the board and executes its directions. In 2009, the RBI arranged to set up the National Payments Corporation of India (NPCI) to act as an umbrella organization for operating various retail payment systems (RPSs) in India. The NPCI is expected to bring greater efficiency by way of uniformity and standardization in retail payments and expanding and extending the reach of both existing and innovative payment products for greater customer convenience.

In addition, the Central Board has three standing committees. The Inspection and Audit Sub-Committee has four non-official Central Board directors, and the Building Sub-Committee and the Staff Sub-Committee have at least two non-official Central Board directors each. There are also four local boards for four regions of the country, each of which has five non-official members, appointed by the government, and a chairman who is one of the directors of the Central Board. The local boards advise the Central Board on matters remitted to them.

In recent years, the conduct of monetary policy has acquired complexity and significance in view of the greater integration with the global economy. Monetary policy refers to the policy of the central bank of the country with regard to the use of monetary instruments under its control to achieve the goals specified in the RBI Act. The RBI is vested with the responsibility of conducting monetary policy as is explicitly mandated under the RBI Act, 1934. The monetary policy framework aims at setting the policy (repo) rate based on an assessment of the current and the evolving macroeconomic situation and modulation of liquidity conditions to anchor money-market rates at or around the repo rate. Repo rate changes are transmitted through the money market to the entire financial system, which, in turn, influences aggregate demand—a key determinant of inflation and growth. The governor of the RBI is the ex-officio chairperson of the Monetary Policy Committee, which meets at least four times a year.

The RBI is accountable to Parliament through the Ministry of Finance, and the governor and the deputy governors appear before parliamentary committees, especially before the Standing Committee on Finance, when called upon to do so. Thus, the formal governance arrangements in the RBI are oriented towards a collegial approach to decision-making. Yet, as in the case of most of the central banks, the governor holds a somewhat unique position in the organization. Convention and tradition do bestow some authority on the governor, commensurate with his unique position. The governor is the public face of the RBI and is generally thought to be accountable for the actions of the Bank.

The governor of the RBI is the chairman of the Central Board and enjoys full powers of superintendence and direction in all the affairs of the Bank. More importantly, he enjoys a privileged position in the financial system. Although the governor has not been accorded any place of significance in the official warrant of precedence, he enjoys a position of great prestige in official functions. The RBI Act does not contain any qualification for the post of governor. As per the provisions of the RBI Act, the acts of the governor on behalf of the Bank cannot be questioned in any court of law.

Role of the Governor

The RBI governor influences a wide range of microeconomic and macroeconomic issues in the country. His signature appears on currency notes and he controls the country's monetary, currency and credit systems. His actions influence not only the entire banking system, but also stock markets, the economy and people's lives at large. It is said that if he sneezes, markets tend to catch a cold! The governor is the sole authority for issuing bank notes. He also oversees all banking operations in the country. He supervises, administers and regulates exchange control and banking operations. Besides administering the government's economic policies, he is responsible for issuing licenses to new banks, both private and foreign. It is the governor who announces the monetary and credit policy twice a year, that is, the slack-season and the busy-season credit policies. Apart from this, there is a bi-monthly policy review, in which inflation, interest rate and money supply in the economy are discussed and open market operations (OMOs) carried out. The RBI's estimation of gross domestic product (GDP) growth in the economy is also announced at the same time.

Apart from the above, the governor also controls the interest rates on advances by prescribing the marginal cost of lending rate (MCLR), which is the reference rate or internal benchmark below which banks are not allowed to lend. He prescribes the minimum cash reserve ratio (CRR) and statutory liquidity ratio (SLR) to be maintained by banks as a ratio of net demand and time liabilities. By making variation in these ratios, the RBI controls the money in circulation with a view to managing the inflation in the economy. He is responsible for ensuring adherence to the provisions of FEMA, 1999. The governor also monitors the issue and exchange (or destruction) of currency and coins unfit for circulation and ensures adequate supply of good quality currency notes and coins to the public.

He is responsible for ensuring that the non-performing assets (NPAs) in the banking sector do not spiral out of control and destabilize the entire banking system. It is his remit to ensure an adequate supply of credit to various sectors of the economy, particularly those with potential for generation of employment to the masses, such as agriculture and the micro, small and medium enterprises (MSME) sectors.

He monitors the implementation of government-sponsored poverty alleviation schemes and is also responsible for maintenance of gold reserves and foreign-exchange reserves of the country.

EIGHTY-SIX YEARS OF THE RBI: AN OVERVIEW

The 86 years of the RBI's existence can be divided into three time periods: before Independence, between Independence and liberalization, and after liberalization. One most important recurring theme that was evident throughout has been independence and autonomy of the RBI vis-à-vis the government.

1935–1947

These first 12 years saw three distinguished governors lead the RBI, only one of them an Indian. Sir Osborne Smith and his successor, Sir James Taylor, were Australian and British, respectively, while the third governor was Sir Chintaman Deshmukh, an Indian. In the initial years, the concerns of the RBI were shaped by its place as a private limited company where British and Indian businessmen were shareholders. The functions associated with a central bank were actually carried out by the Imperial Bank of India, which is now the State Bank of India (SBI). The RBI became the central bank of the country after it was nationalized in 1949. It also served for a brief period as the central bank of Pakistan and Burma (now Myanmar). Admirably, Smith and Taylor, though tasked with protecting British interests, showed great independence in their dealings and tried to understand the aspirations of the people of the country that was on the cusp of gaining independence from foreign rule. Deshmukh, as the first Indian governor, was a legend in his own right and inspired many further governors to assert their independence and integrity.

1947–1992

The years between India gaining independence from the British Empire and the liberalization of the Indian economy saw 15 governors of the RBI. Young India saw near-constant political upheaval, both domestic and international: the devastating partition of India was followed by three wars with Pakistan in 1947, 1965 and 1971; India went to war with China; India was gripped by a devastating famine for three years; Indian democracy saw a long dark time during Emergency and frequent elections and precarious political coalitions meant governments often needed to be bailed out by the RBI. There was no end to the uncertainty, economic and political, that challenged the governors of the institution. It was also the period when the autonomy and the independence of the RBI vis-à-vis the government came to be discussed heatedly due to the Rau–Krishnamachari episode, which culminated in the resignation of Governor Benegal Rama Rau.

1992–present

After liberalization of the Indian economy, the RBI faced new challenges. The years during which liberalization process was undertaken had been turbulent and transformative for India; the country went from being forced to pledge its gold to the International Monetary Fund (IMF) on account of a balance of payments crisis to having huge foreign-exchange reserves of over $638 billion. All through this, the RBI managed to maintain price stability while also focusing on growth. From being a country on the brink of insolvency to one of the fastest-growing economies in the world, India's transformation during this period has been remarkable.

This period saw the relationship between the RBI and the government transform significantly with the passing of the Fiscal Responsibility and Budget Management Act (FRBM), 2003. A landmark in the RBI's history and culmination of the efforts of many successive governors, particularly C. Rangarajan's, Bimal Jalan's and Y.V. Reddy's, this legislation recognized the government's responsibility to maintain financial discipline. The legislation required the government to limit the fiscal deficit to a stipulated percentage of the GDP, so that the RBI did not have to issue ad hoc treasury bills to fund the deficit. This single measure has led to many government initiatives for raising resources and controlling fiscal deficit.

However, this period also saw the relationship between the RBI and the government becoming strained to its very limits sometimes. As the stakes grew higher in an India that was becoming an international economic force to be reckoned with, the relationship between the governor of the RBI and the government grew more important, and it reflected in the improvement of economic decision-making. Governors with bureaucratic experience, like Rangarajan, Jalan and Reddy, had an easier time communicating with the political bosses and bringing about necessary reforms. Governors from academia, like Rajan and Patel, had a harder time accommodating wishes of political masters in their decisions, leading to differences with the government, which resulted in them choosing either to retire instead of accepting extension of their tenure (Rajan) or leave well before their term ended (Patel).

Rajan and Patel, like many other governors of the RBI, are gifted economists and could foresee many of the troubles that would arise in the Indian economy during the process of liberalization, including an enormous increase in NPAs in the banking sector that would not be taken seriously by the government and would lead to destabilization of the entire banking sector. The bold and effective measures they introduced have been carried forward by the present governor, Shaktikanta Das, who had effectively handled the turmoil during demonetization of currency notes in 2016 as secretary of economic affairs in the Ministry of Finance. He ensured India's financial survival through a pandemic (COVID-19) of mammoth proportions. Das rose to the occasion and ably guided India through the unsurmountable difficulties during the pandemic, without losing track of other targets like the recovery of bad debts and corruption in the banking sector.

The last few decades have seen the RBI hog the limelight in a way it never did before the proliferation of media and widespread internet access. The actions of the governors and the policies of the RBI have a far-reaching impact on the daily lives of the masses and the businesses. It is to the credit of the governors, India's unsung heroes, that they continue to work silently, undeterred by the opinions of the masses they serve, who are perhaps unaware that had these gentlemen ignored the gravity of their position and failed in their assigned duties, overall life would have been much miserable.

TRIVIA

1. The state with the largest number of people occupying the seat of the governor is Tamil Nadu (four), while three each were from Maharashtra, Punjab, Andhra Pradesh and West Bengal. Two were from Gujarat and one each from Rajasthan, Bihar, Karnataka, Odisha and Madhya Pradesh. Of the 25, two governors were from other countries (one from Australia and another from Great Britain) and 23 were from India.
2. Sir Benegal Rama Rau enjoyed the longest tenure as the governor of the RBI with seven years and six months, while Amitav Ghosh was the governor for only 21 days.
3. Two of the governors of the RBI later became finance ministers of India. They were Sir C.D. Deshmukh and Dr Manmohan Singh. Dr Singh has the distinction of becoming the prime minister of India twice and has served the country as prime minister from 2004 to 2014.
4. Seven governors resigned during their tenure. Osborne Smith, Benegal Rama Rau and R.N. Malhotra resigned due to differences with the government over policy matters. S. Jagannathan resigned ostensibly to join the IMF as its

executive director, while K.R. Puri was asked to resign due to a change in government. Bimal Jalan resigned as he was elected to the Rajya Sabha and Urjit Patel resigned on personal grounds, but it is widely speculated that he, too, resigned due to differences with the government over policy matters.

1

Sir Osborne Smith

Sir Osborne Arkell Smith, an Australian national who became the RBI's first governor in April 1935, was a veteran banker who had devoted his entire professional life in the service of banking. He spent nearly 20 years in the Bank of New South Wales, Australia's biggest trading bank. Thereafter, he joined the Commonwealth Bank of Australia (CBA), where he served in various important positions for over a decade. The CBA was a bank that undertook both commercial and central bank functions. Though Smith didn't have any formal training in central banking, he did learn the basics at the CBA. He was its London manager when he was chosen by Lord Montagu Norman, the governor of the Bank of England, to join the Imperial Bank of India as a managing governor in 1926. While an Englishman from the Civil Service could have been selected for this job, there was a desire to have someone from outside the government as the first governor, so as to demonstrate the principle of independence of the Bank.

As managing governor, Smith successfully steered the Imperial Bank of India through the Great Depression and also carried out significant reforms for reorganizing its working. He was very reputable as a banker and the choice of Smith as the first governor of the RBI was hailed by the financial and business worlds and the media unanimously. Sir C.D. Deshmukh, the first Indian governor of the RBI, observed:

> Plans, characteristic of the foresight that the British bring to bear on public affairs in order to preserve what they regard as their own legitimate interests, were made to ensure that the first Governor of the Reserve Bank would be a person on whom the Bank of England could rely and of whom they could expect unquestioning co-operation.[1]

However, Smith's stay at the Bank was destined to be a short one. Although his tenure had been fixed at three-and-a-half years, he resigned in October 1936 after only 18 months, citing personal reasons. The Government of India issued the following statement on 30 October 1936:

> The Governor General in Council has received Sir Osborne Smith's application to resign from the Governorship of the Reserve Bank of India. He has accepted it with regret at the loss of an officer who has rendered invaluable service to India, both generally and in the establishment and conduct of the affairs of the Bank. It is with real regret that the Government of India, in deference to his own wish, part with Sir Osborne Smith's great experience and high capacity.[2]

Though Smith resigned in October 1936, his resignation was effective from 1 July 1937. He was given eight months of leave, during which the deputy governor, an Indian Civil Service (ICS) officer, Sir James Taylor, acted as governor. Taylor was appointed governor, effective from 1 July 1937.

Smith's tenure proved to be a controversial one. He had, for long, been critical of the government-recommended 1s. 6d. exchange ratio for the rupee and its deflationary consequences. Press reports also mentioned that Smith had proposed an export duty on gold

---

[1]Simha, S.L.N., *History of the Reserve Bank of India, 1935–51*, Bombay, Reserve Bank of India, 2005, pp. 124–5.

[2]Ibid. 222–3.

to discourage its outflow from India, but the then government opposed it. He was keen on maintaining the independence of the institution he headed. Even in his Imperial Bank days, Smith used to complain of pressures from the government and Secretary of State. Referring to one cablegram from the Secretary of State in 1930, he had remarked that anyone would assume that the Bank was a mere department of the government and he had told the government that as long as he ran the Bank, he would not be run by London or anywhere else and would not tolerate interference in his business. Again, writing to Sir Purshottamdas Thakurdas, a director of the RBI in June 1936, Smith complained that he was 'sick to death of Government's always attempted domination of the Bank.'[3]

According to Deshmukh, the main causes of Sir Osborne Smith's resignation were the serious difference of opinion between him and the then finance member, Sir James Grigg, over the lowering of the bank rate; the temperamental incompatibility with the other deputy governor, Sir James Taylor, and the differences of opinion concerning the exchange rate of the rupee.

But this is only one part of the story. The relations between the governor and Taylor were less than cordial. Smith suspected that, on a number of matters, the deputy governor was dealing directly with the government without his knowledge. It is very probable that the strained relations between Smith and Taylor represented the traditional conflict between professional bankers and Civil Service personnel. Further, Smith was suspected to be soft towards the natives, that is, the Indians.

Although it appeared that Smith resigned due to differences with Grigg, the statement by the government on 30 October 1936 announcing Smith's resignation did not reveal the reasons for his resignation. This issue was raised by a shareholder of

[3]Ibid. 224.

the Bank in its second annual general meeting of the RBI on 8 February 1937, to which the acting governor, Taylor, replied that Smith was retiring for personal reasons. The reasons for his abrupt resignation remained shrouded in mystery even after publication of the *History of the Reserve Bank of India*, Vol. 1, which covered the period of 1935–51 under the guidance of the editorial committee chaired by the third governor of the Bank, Sir C.D. Deshmukh.

In August 2000, Anand Chandavarkar, a renowned author and economist, published a detailed article in the *Economic and Political Weekly*, titled 'Central Bank and Government: An Untold Story from RBI's Early History' after a great deal of research, in which he tried to unravel this mystery. He found that Smith's technical competence was never in doubt but he had legitimate differences over policy issues with Sir James Grigg.[4] Smith strove very hard to preserve autonomy and independence of the RBI and he enjoyed an unusual rapport with and support of the board of directors along with the financial and business communities. However, as a governor, he was guilty of financial malfeasance, reportedly dealing in government securities, along with his cronies in the Bank, on his own account. There was also the other aspect of moral turpitude: He was rumoured to be having an illicit relationship with a certain Mrs Allen, wife of the British manager in the Calcutta office, which soon became talk of the town.

Unfortunately, both episodes resulted in diminishing the stature of the governor's office. To save the image and credibility of the newly established RBI, Lord Montagu Norman worked out a prudent and viable solution of premature and voluntary retirement for Smith. Grigg, too, was no saint. He was guilty of pursuing a sustained and venomous vendetta against Smith ever since the

[4]Chandavarkar, Anand, 'Central Bank and Government: An Untold Story from RBI's Early History', *Economic and Political Weekly*, 5 June 2015, pp. 7–8, http://bit.ly/3lQJINs. Accessed on 14 March 2022.

latter assumed the office of the governor. Further, influencing Smith's deputies, Taylor and Sikandar Hayat Khan, against Smith was an inexcusable breach of conduct and established bureaucratic procedures. His resort to the most intemperate language against Smith was also inexcusable. He resented the RBI's independence even in matters that were specifically in RBI's jurisdiction, such as the bank rate.

Finally, it was Lord Norman's intervention and his solution of early voluntary retirement for Smith that saved the day for the RBI. Smith, on his part, gracefully accepted the solution and resigned, citing health reasons. The issue was swept under the carpet, which was, in a sense, the right thing to do at the time or else the fledgling RBI's reputation would have been tarnished beyond repair. And that was the reason why the entire matter was kept a top secret. Even after 34 years since the episode, *History of the Reserve Bank of India*, first published in 1970, did not make any reference to it.

There is a school of thought that believes that Smith was framed. Within a short time after its establishment, the RBI had established its credentials as an independent and autonomous institution. The need to have Smith as governor no longer existed. He was also proving to be a thorn in the flesh with his insistence on protecting the RBI's autonomy. Moreover, he was sympathetic towards Indians and their aspirations. He had become inconvenient and, therefore, it was necessary to be rid of him. To create the atmosphere for his removal, stories of his alleged illegal liaison with Mrs Allen as well as his financial misdemeanour were planted in the media. It was only because of the support of Lord Norman that he had a safe passage and left the RBI honourably.

Bakhtiar Dadabhoy, whose seminal work *Barons of Banking* covers this controversy in detail, observes that till as late as the early 1990s, there was no portrait of Smith in the boardroom of the Bank.

> By the time the issue of Smith's portrait was examined in the late 1980s, he was long dead. There was a photograph of Smith, which was curiously in the Madras Office of the RBI. It was only during the governorship of S. Venkitaramanan that the issue of Smith's portrait (based on the photograph in the Madras Office) was taken up, and it was in the tenure of his successor, C. Rangarajan, that Smith finally took his rightful place in the portrait gallery of RBI's Governors.[5]

According to Dadabhoy, Smith also enjoys another somewhat-dubious distinction: He is the only governor thus far never to have signed a currency note.

> Actually, Smith had signed a currency note but it was never issued because of the abdication of Edward VII. The [K]ing's abdication delayed the note issues of the bank and the first RBI notes were signed by his successor, Taylor.[6]

[5]Dadabhoy, Bakhtiar K., *Barons of Banking: Glimpses of Indian Banking History*, Noida, Random House India, 2013, pp. 160.
[6]Ibid. 159–60.

2

Sir James Braid Taylor

Sir James Braid Taylor was a senior deputy governor when he was appointed as the second governor of the RBI, after the resignation of Sir Osborne Smith. He was member of the ICS and had worked in the currency department of the Government of India, first as its deputy controller and later as controller of the currency. He had also worked as additional secretary to the finance department. He was not new to the RBI as he was closely associated with the preparation and piloting of the RBI Bill. He was one of the two deputy governors of the Bank since its inception in 1935, the other being Sikandar Hayat Khan. He succeeded to the governorship of the Bank on 1 July 1937.

There were obvious concerns over his appointment concerning the independence of the Central Bank since he was closely associated with the government. He was a very close friend of Sir James Grigg, the finance member. In fact, in British Civil Service Examination of 1913, while Grigg had stood first, Taylor had stood second. Even during the conflict between Grigg and Smith, Taylor had sided with Grigg. Hence, the Indian business and financial community was somewhat sceptical about how the RBI would remain independent under his governorship. After the departure of Smith, who fiercely guarded the independence and autonomy of the Bank, the political and business circles felt that the Bank had become an extension of the government under Taylor. It was during this period that the exchange rate (sterling vs rupee) was fixed at a high of 1s. 6d. to a rupee, which pushed India into deflationary conditions and resulted in deteriorating economic conditions after 1938.

When World War II broke out in 1939, the primary responsibility of the RBI was to help the government manage its finances. The British government wanted the Government of India to support its war-time efforts by meeting some of Britain's shortfall of war-time expenditure. The purchases of war materials and services in India by the Allies resulted in a large accretion of sterling balances, posing problems of utilization in a manner most beneficial to the country. The immediate problems were those of restraining currency expansion, which became automatic on account of the sterling–rupee link, and the upsurge of inflation, compounded by acute shortages of domestic consumption goods and severe contraction of imports. These were the principal matters engaging the attention of the RBI during the War years. However, the RBI met with little success in taming the inflation during that period.

Taylor had maintained excellent relations with the Viceroy's office, the finance member and the entire Central Board of Directors of the RBI. His work as governor was considered to be outstanding enough to be rewarded with an extension of his office for another term of five years, with effect from 1 July 1942, again, on the unanimous recommendation of the Central Board. In the words of one of the Central Board members, C.R. Srinivasan:

> There can be no two opinions on the extension of Sir James Taylor's term. He has acted to the best of his lights in office and the knowledge and experience that he has picked up in the service of the Bank should not be lost to it at a critical occasion like the present.[1]

---

[1]Simha, S.L.N., *History of the Reserve Bank of India, 1935–51*, Bombay, Reserve Bank of India, 2005, p. 269.

His relations with the board of directors were generally cordial and he commanded their respect and willing cooperation, except where, in their opinion, the interests of the country called for disagreement.

The Capital observed:

> [The] Bank possesses a most excellent Governor in Sir James Taylor whose yeoman service from the time when it was nothing more than a scheme on paper and that Sir James Taylor's appointment for a further term of five years is not only testimony to his personal qualities but to the smooth and continuing influence the Bank exercises upon India's economy and the monetary issues that (in the post-[W]ar era) would be resolved realistically, on the basis of past experiences, by him.[2]

It was during this time that it was considered necessary to appoint a deputy to Taylor to be available in case he fell ill or was not in the country. When the search for a suitable European national did not succeed, Taylor suggested the name of Sir C.D. Deshmukh, who was first made the board secretary and was later elevated to the position of deputy governor. Thus, Taylor may be credited to have paved the way for Indianization of the governorship of the RBI. It was during his tenure that 'exchange control' was introduced in India, and the RBI administered the control. Exchange control helped the Bank familiarize itself with the practical operations of the world of international finance. Exchange control department was established in the RBI and authorized dealers were appointed.

It was Taylor who initiated the practice of writing a weekly demi-official letter to the finance secretary in September 1937, containing a brief review of the money, exchange, bullion and commodity markets in India and abroad, apart from the detailed

---

[2]Ibid. 270.

correspondence on specific matters. The practice continued till 1947, long after the demise of Taylor. Unfortunately, he was not destined to continue for long. His was a sudden and premature demise after a short illness on the night of 17 February 1943. His death could not have come at a more inopportune time; the country was beginning to feel deeply the impact of the heavy war expenditures both by the Indian and Allied governments.

His death was widely mourned, and profound regret was expressed at his passing away. The CCB met in a special session on 18 February to pass a condolence resolution. The full board expressed its grief at its meeting on 5 April in the following resolution:

> That the Board record with the profoundest sorrow the premature death of Sir James B. Taylor, the Governor of the Bank, and desire to express their deepest sympathies to Lady Taylor. The Board also wish to pay a tribute of admiration and gratitude to Sir James B. Taylor for the invaluable assistance which he rendered in organising the affairs of the Bank as Deputy Governor and for his masterly handling of them as Governor. They cannot speak too highly of his single-minded devotion to the Bank's interests and the fairness and understanding which invariably characterised his relations with the Board. They mourn the loss of an admirable colleague and consider that, by his death, the Bank has lost an administrator of the highest caliber and India a very good friend.[3]

The untiring efforts put in by Sir James Braid Taylor in shaping the future of the Bank and his warm and considerate nature earned him universal esteem. The kind of respect he had earned can very well be judged from the eulogy given by his trusted

[3]Ibid. 270.

deputy, Sir C.D. Deshmukh, who later followed in his footsteps as governor:

> Sir James Taylor was among the most remarkable men that it has been my good fortune to know. His intelligence was like a lambent flame which illuminated everything that it touched and purged it of dross, and he had a catholicity of interest, a breadth of outlook and a warm humanity which I have seldom seen equalled. His political views were most liberal and fair-minded… It was his firm conviction that the indispensable condition for the achievement and maintenance of self-government for India was a strong, efficient and honest administration through Indian personnel… He was, therefore, an ardent champion of a rapidly progressive Indianisation of the administration with the final goal of complete Indianisation being kept steadily in view. Communalism he regarded as a cancer in the body politic, and it was his opinion that communal electorates must go if there was to be any practical political advance at all in India... In financial matters he was, even in his Controller of the Currency days, a vigilant watch-dog of India's interests.[4]

Sir James Grigg was the finance member of the Government of India during 1934–39. In his autobiography, *Prejudice and Judgment* (J. Cape, 1948), he praised Taylor's skill and tact:

> Incidentally also I had inherited from my predecessor an obligation to set up an Indian Reserve Bank to take over the management of the currency and debt independently of the Government. This I did, but the results were quite other than its promoters intended, for the Central Board was, under the bank's charter, to be mainly elected by the shareholders,

[4]Ibid. 271.

and within four years it came to be dominated by those Hindu big business men who were more than sensitive to suggestions from the Congress caucus, and some of whom had contributed largely to its funds. This might have had serious consequences. That it did not was due very largely to the skill and tact of Sir James Taylor, who was Governor for most of the time I was in India. In addition to his admirably efficient management of the internal affairs of the bank, he showed the utmost loyalty to me, both officially and personally, and we became the firmest of friends. His death during the war was a great grief to me and a severe loss to the bank, though he had trained a gifted Indian deputy who was able to succeed him.[5]

ANECDOTE: THE RBI SEAL

Every institution should have its own unique seal to indicate its status. It is to be used as the emblem of the institution on letterheads and other stationery. In case of a central bank, it is to be used as common seal on currency notes, cheques and other publications, too. Naturally, it was an issue that had to be taken up immediately after the formation of the Bank.

The general ideas on the seal were as follows:

1. The seal should emphasize the governmental status of the Bank, but not too closely.
2. It should have something Indian in the design.
3. It should be simple, artistic and heraldically correct.
4. The design should be such that it could be used without substantial alteration for letter heading, etc.

---

[5]Grigg, James, *Prejudice and Judgment: The Reminiscences of Sir James Grigg*, London, J. Cape, 1948, p. 447.

When various seals, medals and coins were examined for the purpose, the seal of the East India Company, a double mohur with the sketch of a lion and a palm tree, was found to comply with all the above conditions for the Bank's seal. However, it was thought that tiger was a more characteristic animal of India than a lion, and it was decided to replace the lion on the seal with the tiger.

Since there was immediate requirement to issue share certificates of the Bank with its common seal, the work of preparing the seal was entrusted to a Madras firm. The design submitted by the Madras firm was approved by the Bank's board in its meeting on 23 February 1935, but the RBI expressed desire for improvement of the animal's appearance on the seal. The deputy governor, Sir James Taylor, was not satisfied with the image of the tiger on the design. 'The tiger', wrote Taylor, apparently somewhat furiously, 'looks too like some species of dog and I am afraid that a design of a dog under a tree would arouse derision among the irreverent'.[6]

He took keen interest in getting fresh sketches prepared by the Government of India mint and the Security Printing Press, Nasik. However, Taylor could not find anyone to photograph a live tiger. So, he ordered the photographing of the statue of the tiger on the entrance gate at the Belvedere in Calcutta. These sketches also did not satisfy Taylor's desire for a perfect sketch.

A second effort produced better results with the tiger, but the design of the palm tree went wrong. Taylor wrote again, 'The tiger is distinctly good, but the tree has spoiled it. The stem is too long and the branches too spidery, but I should have thought that by putting a firm line under the feet of the tiger and making the tree stronger and lower, we could get quite a good result from the design'.[7]

---

[6]Simha, S.L.N., *History of the Reserve Bank of India, 1935–51*, Bombay, Reserve Bank of India, 2005, p. 132.
[7]Ibid.

After lot of efforts, the Security Printing Press, Nasik, could submit some better proofs. However, it was eventually decided not to make any change in the existing seal of the Bank, and the new sketches came to be used as an emblem for the Bank's currency notes, letterheads, cheques and publications issued by the Bank.

3

Sir C.D. Deshmukh

The first Indian to have occupied the prestigious position of the governor of the RBI was Sir Chintaman Dwarakanath Deshmukh, who was appointed as the governor on 11 August 1943. He remained in office till 30 June 1949. Deshmukh was born on 14 January 1896 at Nata, near Fort Raigarh, in Maharashtra, in a land-holding family with a tradition of public service. His father, Dwarakanath Ganesh Deshmukh, was a respected lawyer, and his mother, Bhagirathibai, was a deeply religious lady.

Deshmukh had an outstanding educational career. He stood first in the matriculation examination of the University of Bombay in 1912 and also secured the first Jagannath Shankarsheth Scholarship in Sanskrit. At the University of Cambridge in 1917, he graduated in the field of Natural Sciences Tripos with Botany, Chemistry and Geology, winning the Frank Smart Prize in Botany. He topped the open competitive examination of the ICS, then held only in London, in 1918. He was probably the youngest among those who held the positions of revenue secretary and finance secretary. Prior to joining the RBI in July 1939, he was the joint secretary to the Department of Education, Health and Lands of the Government of India.

Deshmukh had a career that is perhaps without parallel in modern India. A civil servant, central banker, Union finance minister, educationist, institution builder and social worker, he occupied an amazing array of offices and left an indelible mark on numerous institutions in India. As Bakhtiar Dadabhoy observed:

> The only office that he aspired to, but which eluded him, was that of the President of India. Deshmukh called his memoirs *The Course of My Life*, inviting comparisons between a river and his life. That river originated in the Western Ghats but unlike a normal river, followed a course unprecedented in geography by flowing upward all the time, for the trajectory of his outstanding career knew only one direction, and that was up.[1]

Since setting up of the RBI was being discussed in the late 1920s, there were grave doubts in New Delhi as to how the Bank would evolve. There were fears that the Bank would tilt sympathetically towards Indian nationalist interests. The Bank of England was also worried about its influence over the RBI in the future and, therefore, much depended on the type of person chosen as the governor. Lord Montagu Norman, the governor of the Bank of England, wanted the RBI to be in a position to stand up to a future government dominated by Indians, but did not want it to be in a position to stand up to the Bank of England. He envisaged a gradual tightening and refinement of metropolitan control over Indian monetary policies in the imperial interest.

Deshmukh observed:

> Plans, characteristic of the foresight that the British bring to bear on public affairs in order to preserve what they regard as their own legitimate interests, were made to ensure that the first Governor of the Reserve Bank would be a person

---

[1]Dadabhoy, Bakhtiar K., *Barons of Banking: Glimpses of Indian Banking History*, Noida, Random House India, 2013, pp. 159–60.

> on whom the Bank of England could rely and of whom they could expect unquestioning cooperation.[2]

Obviously, when the RBI was formed, there was no question of any Indian being considered for the post of governor or deputy governor. Taylor, the then deputy governor of the RBI, was looking for 'an Indian who might in due course be found suitable for promotion to one of the two deputy governorships—a man of good general financial knowledge and experience—and from this point of view knowledge of Government finance was nearly as useful as banking or commercial experience—but primarily of energy and administrative capacity and presence'.[3] From as early as 1936, he had set his sights on Deshmukh, who was then serving as finance secretary in the provincial government of Central Provinces and Berar.

When the efforts to get a European deputy governor did not materialize, the Government of India mooted the idea of a liaison officer to be appointed to take charge of the management of the Bank when the governor was away on leave or was indisposed. Taylor suggested Deshmukh's name for the post of liaison officer. The finance member, Sir James Grigg, was initially against it since Deshmukh was a 'Mahratta' and Grigg expected stiff resistance from the board of the RBI, which comprised mostly of businessmen.[4] Further, he also feared that in case of sudden illness or absence of the governor, the management of the Bank would pass on to an Indian, and later, the board could clamour for him to be made governor. However, Taylor managed to persuade Grigg, and Deshmukh's association with the RBI began in July 1939. Three months later, he was appointed as the secretary of

---

[2]Simha, S.L.N., *History of the Reserve Bank of India, 1935–51*, Bombay, Reserve Bank of India, 2005, pp. 124–5.

[3]Ibid. 271–2.

[4]Ibid. 272.

the Central Board of the Bank. While working in this position, he also acted as de facto deputy governor of the Bank. Deshmukh and Taylor formed an excellent pair, and the latter scuttled every move for appointment of a deputy governor, a post which was lying vacant. Due to this, Deshmukh was appointed as the deputy governor in December 1941. As Deshmukh observed, 'Sir James himself deliberately worked towards making me fit to carry the responsibility in succession to himself. He taught me all he knew of Central Banking and the currency and exchange and bullion problems of the country, withheld no confidences and pressed on purposefully with my training.'[5]

With the sudden death of Taylor, the Government of India was caught unawares but did not wish to elevate Deshmukh to be the governor of the Bank. However, the Central Board of the RBI was firmly and unanimously in support of his candidature. After the determined efforts of board members like B.M. Birla and Purshottamdas Thakurdas, Sir C.D. Deshmukh was elevated to the position of governor on 11 August 1943. According to the RBI's official history, Deshmukh's eventual selection was due to 'the rare sense of fair play and statesmanship' displayed by the Secretary of State, L.S. Amery.[6] Although he was a career bureaucrat, Deshmukh was deeply nationalistic. He was advised by none other than Bal Gangadhar Tilak to continue in government service so as to serve the country better when independence came. He was instrumental in designing the federal structure of the country in 1935, having helped prepare the memorandum that shaped the Government of India Act, 1935, which allowed autonomy to the provinces.

When Deshmukh took over as the governor, World War II was at its peak and Bengal was facing one of the worst famines.

---

[5]Ibid. 272–3.

[6]Ibid.

There were severe food shortages since huge supplies were being sent to the Allies in support of the War. Obviously, inflation was uncontrollable. In spite of this, under Deshmukh, the RBI tried to maintain monetary and price stability in the country. During Taylor's governorship, the Exchange Control Department was set up in the RBI, and authorized dealers were appointed to deal in foreign exchange. However, the eligibility conditions were such that only foreign banks were allowed to be authorized dealers. During the tenure of Deshmukh, these conditions were relaxed so as to allow the entry of Indian banks into this highly profitable field. When he was questioned about the change in policy, he pointed out to the government that even sound Indian banks were denied licenses, while such permission was being granted to foreign banks about which the country knew nothing. He opined that promising Indian banks could not be kept away perennially from financing the country's foreign trade. Deshmukh recalled in retrospect years afterwards, 'A private word by me in the ear of the Finance Member that India was the only country in which Government could bring itself to question why a trading privilege had been granted to a national ... proved to be the last word on the subject.'[7]

During the War years, there was a lot of black marketing and hoarding. Therefore, after the War, the government was considering demonetization of high denomination currency notes. The RBI was taken into confidence at a later stage. Deshmukh was not in favour of demonetization and felt that not much could be achieved by the measure. However, the government went ahead with demonetization of high-value currency notes of ₹500 and above, and the ordinance was issued on 12 January 1946. As anticipated by Deshmukh, out of ₹144 crore, ₹135 crore came back into circulation and only ₹9 crore worth of notes were

---

[7]Ibid. 276–7.

extinguished. This episode has relevance even today as has been demonstrated by the poor results of demonetization undertaken by the government in 2016. Apparently, even in 2016, the RBI was not in favour of demonetization.

During World War II, preparations were being made for drawing up of comprehensive plans for post-War monetary cooperation as a result of which the International Monetary Fund (IMF) and the International Bank for Reconstruction and Development (IBRD) (later The World Bank) were established. India was an important member of both the organizations from the beginning. Deshmukh took on a leading role in India's post-War currency plans. He was more concerned about utilization of the huge sterling balances created during the War on account of supply of food, commodities and labour to the Allied Forces for post-War reconstruction, development of the Indian economy and safeguarding its value. He attended the Bretton Woods Conference as a member of the Indian delegation. During this conference, India got the power to nominate an executive director to the IMF. In 1949, Deshmukh chaired the annual meeting of the board of governors of the IMF at Paris.

In 1947, during Partition, the RBI was supposed to give support to the Pakistani government as its central bank and monetary authority till September 1948. Deshmukh persuaded both sides to agree to the RBI to be consulted only in an advisory capacity and not in any partisan manner. However, in spite of the best efforts of the Bank and the governor, mutual distrust and antagonism took its toll and the role of the RBI as the central bank of independent Pakistan was curtailed three months in advance, that is, from 1 July 1948.

At the time of Partition, Pakistan was to be given ₹75 crore as its share and ₹20 crore had already been given. But then Pakistan infringed on the trade standstill agreement by imposing an export duty on jute. It also tried to grab Kashmir. At that time, many felt that it should not be given the remaining ₹55 crore. Deshmukh, however, told the government that an agreement was an agreement and needed to be honoured. The governor behaved in a completely bipartisan manner and ensured that Pakistan received its fair share. In this, he had the full support of Mahatma Gandhi.

It was Deshmukh who foresaw the need for a separate banking legislation for commercial banks as early as in 1943. The Central Board and the government concurred with his views, which set the pace for the renewal of the Bank's efforts for a more comprehensive Act. It laid the foundation for the passage of the Banking Companies Act, 1949 (renamed in 1966 as the Banking Regulation Act, after the provisions of the Act were made applicable to the cooperative banks).

He presided over the transformation of the RBI from a private shareholders' bank to a nationalized institution. He also secured the enactment of a comprehensive legislation for the regulation of banking companies and the establishment of the first financial institution for the provision of long-term credit to industries, namely, the Industrial Finance Corporation of India (IFCI). He also initiated a number of steps for building up adequate machinery for rural credit. One of his outstanding contributions to the RBI was the substantial reorganization of the various sections of the Agricultural Credit Department in August 1945. Deshmukh, as governor of the RBI and head of the India delegation, attended the Savannah Conference that ratified the establishment of the IMF and IBRD at Wilmington Island, Savannah, USA, in March 1946. He played a very important role in establishing sound traditions of international monetary cooperation. During the course of the debate in the Legislative Assembly, tributes were paid to the governor for his work at Savannah.

His term ended on 10 August 1948 and the Central Board of the RBI as well as the government were keen to ensure his continuation as governor. However, Deshmukh was not inclined to continue due to personal reasons. However, he agreed to continue till June 1949, during which he oversaw the smooth passage of the Reserve Bank (Transfer to Public Ownership) Act, 1948, thereby nationalizing this august institution. In a resolution passed at its meeting held on 13 June 1949, the Central Board praised the extraordinary services rendered by Deshmukh to the country and his 'high standard of efficiency, integrity and impartiality'. It was hoped that he would put his 'great ability, administrative capacity and high sense of duty' at the disposal of the country for any responsible work he might be invited to undertake in future, and prayed that 'he may live long to distinguish himself further in the service of the motherland as one of the most noble and gifted sons of India'.[8]

Prime Minister Jawaharlal Nehru asked Deshmukh to work on the organization of the Planning Commission and appointed him as a member. Shortly thereafter, he joined the Union Cabinet as the finance minister and held that office with distinction until he resigned in July 1956. It is said that Deshmukh resigned as the finance minister in 1956 in protest over Nehru making Bombay the bilingual capital of Gujarat and Maharashtra as also to protest against the police firing on protesters demanding 'Samyukta Maharashtra'.

Deshmukh was the president of the Indian Statistical Institute (ISI) from 1945 to 1964. It was during this period when he was both the president of the ISI and the Union finance minister that the National Sample Survey was instituted (1951–52) and the Central Statistics Office was established. He was the president of the Institute of Economic Growth, New Delhi, from 1965 to 1974. He served as the honorary chairman of the National Book Trust from 1957 to 1960. He founded the India International Centre in 1959, of which he was the life president. He headed the

---

[8]Ibid. 496–8.

board of governors of the Administrative Staff College of India, Hyderabad, from 1959 to 1973, and was also the chairman of the Indian Institute of Public Administration, New Delhi, in 1963–64.

Deshmukh also made significant contributions to the formulation and implementation of the country's First and Second Five Year Plans. He also played a very important role in the enactment of a new Companies Act, and nationalization of the Imperial Bank of India (now the SBI) and life insurance companies. He was chairman of the University Grants Commission from 1956 to 1960, helping to lay a solid foundation for the improvement of the standards of university education in the country. He was the vice-chancellor of the University of Delhi from March 1962 to February 1967, building it up as an outstanding institution for higher learning. He was a co-recipient of the Ramon Magsaysay Award for distinguished government service in 1959. A number of prestigious universities and institutions, international as well as Indian, conferred on him honoris causa doctorates; these included the Universities of Princeton (USA), Leicester (UK), Pune, Delhi, Allahabad, Nagpur and Osmania (India) as well as the ISI.

He was married to Rosina, an Englishwoman, who passed away in 1949. In 1953, he married Durgabai, equally eminent in her own right. Their joint contribution in the field of functional literacy and family-planning work undertaken by the Andhra Mahila Sabha, of which Durgabai was the founder president, was outstanding. Deshmukh and his wife were both awarded the Padma Vibhushan in 1975, the only instance of a husband–wife team being honoured so.[9]

Deshmukh had a great love for gardening and horticulture was his special hobby. His love for Sanskrit is well known and he published a volume of his poems in Sanskrit in 1969. Deshmukh

---

[9]Dadabhoy, Bakhtiar K., *Barons of Banking: Glimpses of Indian Banking History*, Noida, Random House India, 2013, p. 75.

was also a linguist. He was proficient in Sanskrit, Bengali, Gujarati, Urdu, Marathi, Hindi and English. After his marriage to Durgabai, he also picked up some Telugu. He also knew French; at the annual meeting of the IMF and the World Bank held in Paris in 1950, he gave a speech in French, something that immediately endeared him to his hosts. Deshmukh also enjoyed the unique distinction of operating a personal current account with the RBI. A letter written by him to the manager of the RBI in Hyderabad in June 1976 asking to credit a cheque to his account with them is on display at the RBI Archives in Pune. Deshmukh passed away in Hyderabad on 2 October 1982, at the age of 86.[10]

TRIVIA

1. The finance secretary and the economic advisor were not in favour of the elevation of Sir C.D. Deshmukh from deputy governor to the position of governor. When his elevation to the governorship became certain, the finance department went so far as to suggest that in every important case, the governor should also ascertain the opinion of the managing director of the Imperial Bank. This practice was soon abandoned.
2. Deshmukh enjoyed the unique distinction of operating a personal current account with the RBI. A letter written by him to the manager of the RBI in Hyderabad in June 1976, asking to credit a cheque to his account with them, is on display at the RBI Archives in Pune.

[10]Ibid. 76.

4

Sir Benegal Rama Rau

Sir Benegal Rama Rau was the fourth governor of the RBI from 1 July 1949 to 14 January 1957. Rau came from an extremely distinguished family. His elder brother, Benegal Narasing Rau, was a High Court judge and diplomat who was instrumental in framing the Constitution of India. His younger brother, Benegal Shiva Rau, was a politician who would eventually edit the debates in the Constituent Assembly. Rau completed his education from the Universities of Madras and Cambridge. He later joined the ICS in 1913.

Rau had a distinguished career. He was India's ambassador to the USA before he was appointed as the governor of RBI. He held several important positions during his career, including secretary to the Indian Taxation Enquiry Committee, financial advisor to the Simon Commission, deputy high commissioner for India in London, chairman of the Bombay Port Trust and ambassador for India in the USA. As secretary of the Indian delegation to the Round Table Conference and the Joint Parliamentary Committee (JPC), he had actively participated in the discussions on the question of establishing a central bank for India in the early 1930s. Early in May 1949, the government also nominated him as the director of the Central Board of the Bank. When his appointment as the governor was announced, he worked as Sir C.D. Deshmukh's understudy for a few months so as to get acquainted to his duties as the governor of the RBI.

Rau knew well the importance of audit and inspection, and the early months of his tenure saw him devote considerable energy to organize the RBI's inspection activities. He was also cautious about expenditure and made the decision to sell the governor's residence in Calcutta as an austerity measure. Since the Japanese invasion of Burma (now Myanmar) in 1942, which brought the World War II to India's backyard if not India's doorsteps, the RBI had maintained two residences for the governor: one in Calcutta and one in Bombay. Long after the War ended, the governors continued to operate only from Bombay. Seeing no use in maintaining a residence that would not be used, the Calcutta residence was sold in December 1949.

Much of the RBI's work in the years Rau was the governor reflects the needs and priorities of young India. In accordance with the recommendations of the Rural Banking Enquiry Committee, the Department of Banking Development (DBD) was set up in October 1950. It was to deal with the development of banking and credit facilities in the country and give specific and dedicated attention to the extension of banking facilities to semi-urban areas and to the problems of rural finance. The department was also expected to deal with other matters such as the financing of MSMEs and the establishment of state industrial finance corporations.

The Report of the All-India Rural Credit Survey Committee 1954 proposed that the Imperial Bank of India be nationalized and entrusted with the responsibility to spread banking facilities to the remote regions of the country. The committee also recommended the formation of a new bank, the SBI, by amalgamating the Imperial Bank of India with the 10 major banks associated with the former princely states. The 10 major state-associated banks were the State Bank of Saurashtra, Bank of Patiala, Bank of Bikaner and Jaipur, Bank of Rajasthan, Bank of Indore, Bank of Baroda,

Bank of Mysore, Hyderabad State Bank and Travancore Bank. It was proposed that the SBI would be mainly for extending modern banking to the rural areas and linking it with the needs of cooperative credit and marketing institutions.

Deshmukh, as finance minister in the Nehru Cabinet, was quite keen on extending financial assistance to rural areas. Thus, at his behest, particularly 1951 onwards, the RBI's interest in rural finance was intensified. The scale of the Bank's financial assistance to the cooperative movement also recorded a marked expansion. With a view to enhance the rural credit, Rau formed the All-India Rural Credit Survey Committee and, based on the committee's recommendations, proposed to the government that an 'SBI' be formed by merging the Imperial Bank of India, the 10 large state-associated banks and four small state-associated banks. That led to nationalization of the Imperial Bank of India on 30 April 1955, and thus began the journey of the SBI on 1 July 1955.

The government was in favour of an immediate merger of all the state-associated banks with the newly formed SBI. However, Rau was in favour of a gradual merger of all state-associated banks, so as to ensure that the process is completed without any hiccups. He believed that it might be impractical to integrate the Imperial Bank with the other state-associated banks, which differed significantly in their character and culture, in one quick and comprehensive operation. He proposed that the Imperial Bank should first be reconstituted, and, thereafter, the other banks should be taken up for reconstitution and merger. Rau emphasized that it would guard against any abrupt increase in establishment costs and allow a lengthy interval to assimilate the policies of the smaller banks into those of the Imperial Bank of India.

Somehow, Rau's views prevailed over those in favour of immediate integration of all the state-associated banks with the Imperial Bank to form the SBI. The government heeded Rau's advice since the reorganization of states was also ongoing at that time. Hence, instead of direct merger, the state-associated banks (Hyderabad, Patiala, Saurashtra, Indore, Travancore, Bikaner and Jaipur and Mysore) were converted into subsidiaries of the SBI, keeping their independent status alive by making them wholly-owned associate banks of the SBI. (State Bank of Bikaner and Jaipur [SBBJ], State Bank of Mysore [SBM], State Bank of Travancore [SBT], State Bank of Hyderabad [SBH] and State Bank of Patiala [SBP] have been recently merged with the SBI, from 1 April 2017, along with the Bharatiya Mahila Bank [BMB]). The importance of Rau's reasoning should be seen in the context of the dithering of the government for almost 62 years before the associate banks were finally merged with the SBI in 2017.

A full-fledged office of the Issue Department was established in Delhi and its sub-office was established at Gauhati. Note Cancellation Sections were also set up at several places in the country. Further, a full-fledged legal division was set up in the central office in April 1950 to take care of various complex legal issues the Bank was facing in the discharge of its statutory functions as well as during the course of integration of various princely states with Union of India and extension of the RBI Act to them. The post of executive director was created during his tenure to take care of the increasing workload and to ensure proper delegation of work.

Knowing fully well the importance of deficit financing in a growing nation like India, the RBI undertook first deficit financing of the government in 1951 for the first time. The Bank rate as an effective tool of monetary policy was revived since November 1951, and it was used as a tool to control any inflationary effects of the deficit financing. By doing so, it effectively established itself as the sole monetary authority having control over the banking sector in India. It is interesting to note that in earlier years, that is, from 1935 to 1951, the Imperial Bank of India was competing with the RBI in providing accommodation to commercial banks, which rendered it less effective as the controlling authority.

Apart from this, under Rau, the RBI also took special interest in the management of debt financing of the newly organized states. The experience of the officials at the Bank with regard to the use of overdraft facility by states was very disappointing. Hence, the Bank used a variety of means, ranging from formal approaches to informal links with officials of state governments, to urging the latter to 'keep a vigilant eye on their ways and means position'.[1] Later on, the Bank produced a formidable body of work on the finances of state governments. This work has continued even today as a result of the close interest the Bank has taken in the financial problems of state governments and has given them unmatched expertise on this subject.

Rau took a special interest in the Bill Market Scheme, which was introduced in January 1952 with the aim to provide eligible banks a mechanism that they could use to obtain advances from the RBI against specially created bills arising out of bona fide commercial or trade transactions, having a maturity not exceeding 90 days. It was a step towards creating a bill market in India and relieving seasonal stringency in the money markets. Greater elasticity in the seasonal expansion and contraction of credit was an objective of the Bill Market Scheme. The RBI hoped that the banks placing greater reliance on advances from it would lead to more frequent contacts with them and would be conducive to 'better mutual understanding ... in the context of the responsibilities placed on the banking system in the Five Year Plan'.[2] It was speedily pushed by Rau in the face of stringent opposition from Department of Banking Operations (DBO) at the RBI. The scheme was welcomed wholeheartedly by the market. The scheme represented the 'first planned steps for a bill market'

---

[1]Balachandran, G., *The Reserve Bank of India: 1951–1967*, Mumbai, Oxford University Press, 1998, p. 194.

[2]Ibid. 54–63.

as remarked by the *Indian Finance*. The journal also remarked that Rau had demostrated accurate insight into the needs of monetary institutions.[3] However, various flaws cropped up in the working of the scheme, and it became unviable after the government increased the stamp duty on negotiable bills from 1957.

By 1955, stagnating growth and deteriorating external finances resulted in increasing deficit financing. To tide over the temporary cash flow mismatches, in May 1955, the RBI and the Ministry of Finance endorsed a new mechanism by which the cap of three months on ways and means advances lent by the RBI to the government was dispensed with. The long-standing nature of the new arrangement resulted in burgeoning deficit financing in later years. Rau and the RBI could not visualize the blatant misuse of the arrangement by the government to its advantage by obtaining cheap credit from the RBI. It also weakened the bargaining power of the RBI vis-à-vis the Ministry of Finance as the RBI surrendered a vital element of monetary control with this single imprudence. This arrangement resulted in disregard of fiscal prudence at the Centre but also emboldened states to run huge overdrafts that had to be taken over by the central government.

The years between 1953 and 1956 were relatively calm for Rau. It was in 1957 that industrial and financial policies in India took a sharp curve towards the left, leaving Rau reeling and ultimately forcing him to resign from the RBI. It is worth examining what pushed Rau to resign. Under the RBI Act, the RBI is subject to the control of the central government. In the early years of the RBI, the government's control was not bothersome. But the events of 1956–57 highlighted clearly that it was possible for a powerful and wily finance minister to subordinate the will of the RBI to his own. Rau's disagreements with the then finance minister T.T. Krishnamachari directly culminated in his resignation from the

---

[3]Ibid. 59.

RBI, and Prime Minister Nehru's refusal to help Rau assert the autonomy of the RBI did not help matters.

The RBI had, until then, enjoyed considerable autonomy under Deshmukh. This was not to say that he and Rau had been the closest of friends, but they had been cordial and cooperative with each other. As finance minister, Deshmukh could be sensitive to the RBI's criticism, but there was an unquestionable underlying respect for the RBI as an institution and its autonomy. Even though Rau's relationship with Deshmukh had been strained towards the end of the latter's tenure because of Rau's opposition to taking over state-associated banks, both the RBI and Rau had been assured of their position while Deshmukh was finance minister. But in July 1956, Deshmukh resigned from the Cabinet in protest against the police firing in Bombay, which had been targeted at the protesters of the Samyukta Maharashtra Committee. The protest was organized to object to the government's proposal to carve out Bombay as a separate union territory. Krishnamachari was appointed to fill the vacancy left behind after Deshmukh's resignation.

Rau's enthusiasm for his job had waned over the years, and Krishnamachari did not do much to make him feel secure. Both Rau and Krishnamachari were intelligent men with impeccable credentials, but the latter treated the RBI as his sidekick and the former as a consistent annoyance. Rau's letters to Nehru and Krishnamachari show his ire at the repeated disrespect he faced, which began within a few weeks of Krishnamachari assuming office. Their differences came into the open over the busy-season credit policy in August 1956, when Krishnamachari, in Rau's presence, announced a monetary policy stance that differed from the one signalled by the RBI. This encroachment on his domain hurt the governor and lowered the prestige of the RBI in public. There were other tiffs: for instance, to replace the cess fund scheme for the handloom sector, Rau had circulated a note over a scheme of time-bound support for the sector, administered through institutional financing agencies. Krishnamachari was in favour of the cess fund scheme but took serious exception to the note. He objected to the note, which quoted his remarks to the Cabinet in a way that, he felt, misrepresented his thoughts.

Krishnamachari's behaviour was the straw that broke the camel's back for Rau long before matters became truly ugly. It began with the new finance minister, T.T. Krishnamachari, presenting the central budget, where he had raised the stamp duty on bills of exchange. This amounted to an increase in the interest rate. Krishnamachari had not considered it necessary to consult the RBI on the matter except to ask if the new rate should be 40 times the old one or 80, offending Rau. The bill market was his pet project and this new measure had killed it. Rau protested the new measure, percieving it as the finance minister overstepping into the governor's domain. Krishnamachari paid no heed to Rau's protests, and so Rau brought his grievance to the prime minister. The prime minister put the case to the Cabinet at a meeting Rau was invited to attend, but upon arrival, Rau found he was unwelcome and not permitted to speak as he was not a member of the Cabinet. He had been invited for an interrogation, not a mutually fruitful discussion. Rau felt insulted and rattled at the implication that the RBI was subordinate to the government and required to heed when ordered by the Ministry of Finance. Worse, the finance minister declared in Parliament that the proposed hike was a 'fiscal measure with monetary intent'.[4]

Reportedly, Rau met with the finance minister to discuss this issue and could not tolerate the derogatory way he referred to the RBI as a department or section of the Ministry of Finance. He pointed out that while the government had powers under Section 7 of the RBI Act to issue directions to the RBI in public

[4]Ibid. 717.

interest after consulting the governor, there had never been any need to use these powers because the government and the RBI worked harmoniously and respectfully to achieve their goals. Having asserted the responsibilities and position of the RBI, Rau approached the Central Board to send the government a memorandum gently reminding them to consult the RBI on matters that significantly affected monetary policy and structure.[5]

In truth, Rau wanted to resign. However, he stayed his hand after long consultations with Prime Minister Nehru and Home Minister G.B. Pant. Instead he decided to speak to Krishnamachari and issue the memorandum. It was received as poorly as one might expect: Nehru told Rau that it was improper, agitational and inappropriate to make public the details of a private conversation he had with Krishnamachari. Curiously, Nehru suggested that the RBI's policies were contrary to those of the government, and that it would be absurd if the RBI followed a different policy just because it disagreed with the government's objectives as laid out in the Five-Year Plans and methods of achieving them. He criticized the RBI for 'encouraging and indirectly participating' in the criticism of the government, leaving Rau stunned.[6] Any impression he had had a week ago that Nehru was sympathetic to his concerns had been obliterated. Interestingly, a fortnight later, Nehru would admit in a letter to Vaikunthlal Mehta, a well known co-operator and vice chairman of the SBI, that the matter may have been handled poorly by the government and that the governor of the RBI should have been consulted before the Cabinet decided to raise stamp duty, but he conveyed none of this to Rau himself.

Soon after this, Nehru left for a prolonged overseas tour. Emboldened in his absence, Krishnamachari intensified pressure

---

[5]Ibid. 720.

[6]Ibid. 721.

on the RBI. He had accused and criticized the RBI over different matters, unhindered by time or place: Parliament was as much fair game as the Southern Indian Chamber of Commerce in Madras. There was no longer any holding back for either him or Rau, who wrote an 11-page reply to Nehru that conveyed his confusion and distress. The definite intent of the RBI Act was to set up an autonomous body, and this objective had been reiterated in 1949 when the RBI was nationalized, so why was Nehru supporting Krishnamachari's stance? Rau also objected to Nehru's allegations of the RBI challenging the government's policies, defending the RBI's record regarding both monetary stability and its support of the government's goals for development. Finally, he sought Nehru's permission to resign, as he could no longer continue in office.

Perhaps already reconciled to losing Rau, Nehru did not cede an inch. He maintained that the memorandum was improperly worded, and advised Rau to view Krishnamachari's actions in the context. Of course, the RBI was a part of the various activities of the government, with high status and responsibility. But even as it had to advise the government, it had to keep in line with it.[7]

In his resignation letter, dated a week before he vacated office on 14 January 1957, Rau reiterated his position. He protested Krishnamachari's remarks against the RBI, calling them 'unwarranted and insulting'.[8] He stressed that the RBI had maintained its independence even while enjoying cordial relations with the finance ministry in the past. It was Krishnamachari's 'personal rudeness' that he had overlooked in the past but he could no longer accept his public attacks on the RBI. At the same time, he wrote a letter to Nehru that implied he was eager to leave the matter behind, choosing not to issue any public statement unless

[7]Ibid. 722.

[8]Ibid. 723.

there was further provocation, as this public discord could have repercussions both in India and abroad.

Rau's resignation marked the end of an important period in the RBI's history. It proved beyond a shadow of doubt that no governor could hope to defend the autonomy of the RBI by announcing its independence. The RBI had also seen a steady rise in its public and policy profile during Rau's tenure, and he had been keen to promote and protect that profile. He had sacrificed his office in defense of the RBI's independence, as he played a major role in safeguarding its autonomy since its nationalization in 1949. The story of Rau and Krishnamachari has descended into folklore, and every governor since Rau has been evaluated by a new criterion: their ability to protect the RBI's autonomy. Amusingly, in his second term as finance minister, Krishnamachari declared in the Lok Sabha in April 1964 that he was 'very happy that successive governors of the RBI … are able to take an independent view and do not completely subordinate their views to those of the party in power, including the Minister.'[9] He even exhorted the RBI to keep on exercising that independence.

---

[9]Ibid. 725–6.

5

K.G. Ambegaokar

The fifth governor of the RBI was Krishnanath Ganesh Ambegaokar, a member of the ICS who had served as finance secretary before his appointment as deputy governor of the RBI. He was appointed governor after Sir Benegal Rama Rau resigned and held this post for 45 days, from 14 January to 28 February 1957. Apart from Sir Osborne Smith and Amitav Ghosh, Ambegaokar is the only other RBI governor whose signature does not appear on any Indian rupee notes and his tenure was the shortest after those of B.N. Adarkar and Amitav Ghosh. Despite this, he made noteworthy contributions to the future of the RBI.

Ambegaokar forged closer connections between the RBI and agricultural enterprises in India. His involvement in facilitating the link between the RBI and Indian agricultural enterprises dated back to April 1935, when his experience as senior deputy registrar of cooperative societies in the Central Provinces and Berar led to his appointment as officer-in-charge of the newly established Agricultural Credit Department. The department began to function immediately with a skeletal staff, and one of its first tasks was to study the Darling report on cooperative credit. Ambegaokar also foresaw the need for legislation banning acceptance of public deposits by companies, which resulted in appropriate restrictive clauses being incorporated in the Companies Act, 1956.

An interesting exchange from Ambegaokar's time as joint secretary to the finance department reflects his commitment to the RBI. There were certain misgivings in some quarters about the role of the RBI in developing the bill market as well as the RBI's failure to report its views on a permanent basis for the Indian monetary system. Other criticisms were about the establishment of links with indigenous bankers, non-improvement of the machinery for dealing with agricultural finance and non-assistance to banks that worked on unsound lines. The demand for nationalization of the RBI began to gain strength. On 18 February 1947, Tamizuddin Khan moved a resolution in the Legislative Assembly recommending that the RBI be taken over by the government, converted into a state bank and run as such. He felt that the monetary organization of the country should be a national concern rather than being confined to a limited number of shareholders that represented capitalism, as the RBI was then a limited company.

Finance Member Liaquat Ali Khan felt that when allegations were made against the RBI, it was only fair that somebody should defend the RBI before the House. Participating in the debate at his request, Ambegaokar not only defended the RBI strongly but also stressed that the RBI had been in existence for a very short time and that within five years of its establishment, World War II had broken out. In response to the criticism that the RBI 'printed a lot of money' and helped inflation, Ambegaokar remarked that the RBI was not to be blamed, as its hands were tied under the Act.[1]

Winding up the debate, Liaquat observed that it was evident that there was a general desire for the nationalization of the RBI. While the government was in favour of nationalizing any institution if such a step would benefit the country, the government would

---

[1]Simha, S.L.N., *History of the Reserve Bank of India, 1935–51*, Bombay, Reserve Bank of India, 2005, p. 511.

study carefully and sympathetically the proposition contained in Tamizuddin's resolution. Thus concluded K.G. Ambegaokar's role in the nationalization of the RBI.[2]

ANECDOTE: THE HUMBLE PIE[3]

For much of the nineteenth century, the pie was the smallest minted coin in India. It constituted one-third of a pice and was officially termed one-twelfth of an anna. Three pies made a pice, four pice made an anna and 16 annas made a rupee. Thus, one rupee consisted of 192 pies. (No wonder arithmetic daunted the fainthearted then!) In the wake of World War II, India witnessed an inflationary situation as well as a scarcity of metals that had to be imported. It was in this context of rising prices that minting of copper pie was discontinued after 1942. Ten years later, there was a proposal by the mint master that the pie be reintroduced as a part of the coinage of the Republic of India. The proposal, however, was very gently quashed by the then finance secretary, K.G. Ambegaokar, who later also served as the governor of the RBI in 1957, on cost benefit considerations. Sir C.D. Deshmukh, the former governor of the RBI, was then the finance minister. He had the last word, ending the saga of the humble pie.

Ambegaokar stated, 'Much as I admire the valiant efforts made to rescue the "picayune coin", I must, I am afraid, albeit with a heavy heart, write:

[2]Ibid. 510–13.

[3] Adapted from 'Anecdote 1–The Humble Pie,' *Reserve Bank of India*, http://bit.ly/3KOzl7B. Accessed on 10 February 2023.

The Epitaph of the Pie

Low and high
We all will sigh
When the poor little pie
Bids her last goodbye.
But her cost's is so high;
And what can she buy?
What trade can she ply?
She needs must eat the humble pie;
So let us not vie
To keep alive the pie
And without a plaintive cry
Peacefully let her die.
If you want the reason why
There need not be hue and cry
Remember she'll in honour lie
With the silver rupee high!
Will the 'Minister' say the last word?

K.G. Ambegaokar
Secretary
12 July 1952

In the note, C.D. Deshmukh concurred, stating:

Let not the 'press' of men
Disturb a museum piece
When life's extinct, oh then
The pie shall lie in peace.

C.D. Deshmukh
13 July 1952

6

H.V.R. Iengar

Haravu Venkatanarasingha Verada Raj Iengar was the sixth governor of the RBI. He was a member of the ICS and had served as the principal private secretary to Pandit Nehru when he was the prime minister. He had also briefly served as the chairman of the SBI, during which period he successfully began the task of orienting the former Imperial Bank towards non-traditional banking goals. He was appointed as the sixth governor of the RBI on 1 March 1957 and held the post till 28 February 1962.

Iengar came to the RBI with something of a crusader's spirit. The Bank steadily expanded its commitments and widened the scope of its engagement with a variety of agencies during the Iengar years. However, the later years of Iengar's tenure were marked by a desire to consolidate rather than to expand.

Iengar was the then finance minister T.T. Krishnamachari's personal choice for the position of the governor of the RBI. Iengar had worked closely with the finance minister when the latter was in the commerce and industry ministry. In spite of Krishnamachari's mercurial nature, Iengar appeared to have cordial relations with him and was expected to handle him better. When Iengar's name was making the rounds for being appointed as the governor, considering his closeness to Krishnamachari, people did not expect him to be significantly independent from the finance ministry.

Iengar, for his part, was aware of the strengths and weaknesses of the finance minister and did not mind using that knowledge when necessary. When he was the chairman of the SBI, he had lost no time in investigating the complaint from Krishnamachari about the RBI having denied accommodation to a South Indian company specializing in the hire-purchase financing of trucks. On the other hand, as the governor of the RBI, Iengar displayed considerable firmness in rejecting Krishnamachari's allegations against the RBI inspectors that they had acted unfairly in pulling up a South Indian bank for having made advances to a prominent newspaper group against the pledge of its immovable property.

Due to the cordial relations between the governor and the finance minister, normalcy returned to the relations between the RBI and the Ministry of Finance, which had been strained considerably during the stormy period when Sir Benegal Rama Rau was the governor and Krishnamachari was the finance minister. It is worth noting that the latter aired his views to Iengar on relatively routine aspects of the RBI's functioning in a manner he might not have done with his predecessor (Sir Benegal Rama Rau). The finance minister's capacity for 'inspiration, grasp, and drive' was believed to have the effect of producing in his officials a 'blind sense of loyalty'. Whether blind or not, Krishnamachari obviously did not suspect Iengar's loyalty.[1]

Iengar was affable, accessible and encouraged debate within the organization. He was effective and vigorous as the governor. But people could see a marked change in the tone of the RBI in its relations with the government after Iengar took over. This is reflected in the speech C.H. Bhabha, then chairman of the Indian Banks' Association, made to the annual general meeting of March 1958. He spoke of the 'impression ... prevailing ...

---

[1]Balachandran, G., *The Reserve Bank of India: 1951-1967*, Mumbai, Oxford University Press, 1998, p. 726.

despite all official and Ministerial assurances [to the contrary of a] certain amount of subservience of the Reserve Bank to the Finance Ministry of the Government of India'. Declaring that all knowledgeable people 'longed' for this 'key institution' to maintain a 'sturdy independence', Bhabha called for changes in the way the RBI's Central Board was constituted and a 're-enunciation of its autonomy'. He also proposed that the RBI should revive the tradition of 'effectual and highly critical review of economic conditions' and policies for which it was known before it became a 'state-owned organisation'.[2]

Iengar was more dynamic and energetic than Rau was in his later years in office and was keener to mark a presence on a wider stage. He had felt restricted at the SBI. Hence, he tried to increase his horizon by keeping in regular touch with the finance ministry, various ministers, the prime minister and bureaucrats. His excellent interpersonal relations with ministers and officials proved to be useful to the Bank on more than one occasion. However, in the bargain, he appeared to have compromised the autonomy and independence of the very organization he was supposed to protect. The political class had become brazen and assertive vis-à-vis various public institutions, and this change was overlooked by Iengar in his efforts to ensure RBI shed its aloofness.

Rau cherished the way traditional central banking was done and found it difficult to manage the changing political and economic decision-making, in contemporary India. Iengar, on the other hand, justified the RBI's descent into the real arenas of economic decision-making, as he appeared to have judged that the RBI gained additional influence and leverage thereby. It appears that a major concern for Iengar was to transform the RBI into an institution that strove continually to be relevant to the economic

[2]Ibid. 727.

challenges facing the country rather than institutional autonomy. Iengar was more realistic, as he could see the changing tides. During Rau's tenure, the RBI was the only institution having a full-fledged economic analysis and research department in India. Its views were frequently sought on economic matters while taking major policy decisions and were respected. By the time Iengar became the governor, however, the analysis and policy landscape had been greatly transformed. The Planning Commission set up in 1950 had meanwhile grown enormously in stature and influence. And this think-tank was closer to the corridors of economic and political decision-making in Delhi than the RBI.

In early 1957, Iengar was concerned that the creation of ad hoc treasury bills had become a mechanical affair and that no checks existed on the government's ability to spend. This was a recipe for disaster. 'As matters now stand,' the governor declared, 'with an automatic expansion of currency at the will of Government, the Bank ... is not really in a position to discharge ... [the] responsibility [vested in it by statute of regulating] the issue of bank notes ... with a view to securing monetary stability in India.'[3]

Even the states were borrowing rampantly from the RBI for their development needs, which resulted in inflation going out of control. Hence, Iengar told the Centre that a situation had now been reached in which 'the states and the Centre must take concerted action in the matter of raising loan resources'. He advised Krishnamachari to convene a conference of few finance ministers and the RBI to discuss the issue. The conference was convened in Bombay in June 1957. This conference is famous, not for what it achieved but what transpired outside it. During adjournment of its proceedings, Krishnamachari had purportedly given his consent to investing the funds of the Life Insurance Corporation (LIC; which was a subsidiary of the RBI that time)

---

[3]Ibid. 39–40.

in Haridas Mundhra's concerns, which were undergoing financial troubles and went bust later on. It became a huge scandal that engulfed even the RBI. Iengar had to appear before the Chagla Committee, formed under the chairmanship of Justice M.C. Chagla by Parliament to investigate into the scandal. Krishnamachari had to ultimately resign as finance minister. This episode not only diminished Iengar's stature as governor within the RBI and in the financial community but also diminished the stature of the RBI as the supreme financial institution in the country. The episode mandated a review of the RBI's functions, which resulted in a Central Board memorandum on the subject which concluded that the Bank's 'functions should not be so diffused as to jeopardize its ability to carry out its primary responsibility as the monetary authority of the country'.[4]

It is interesting to note that Krishnamachari had suggested to Iengar in April 1957 that the RBI should be a monitoring agency for the stock exchanges, and entire control and regulation that was being exercised by the government so far should be vested with the RBI. However, considering his own personal experience during the Haridas Mundra affair, Iengar realized that the Bank would land into avoidable controversies if it gets into the government's shoes in this regard. He suggested that the government should nominate its own officers to the stock, bullion and commodity exchanges rather than those of the Bank, and it was finally accepted by the government. Further, an amendment bill was on the anvil at this time to constitute an investment board of the LIC with the governor of the RBI as its chairman. That was also abandoned by the government at the request of the Bank itself. Considering what happened in 1992 and 2002, one can see how correct Iengar's assessment was.[5]

[4]Ibid. 1,166.

[5]Ibid. 794–807.

Bad loans have always been a never-ending headache for the RBI. Over the years, many banks have gone bust and many new have come up. Since there was no regulation, free entry and exit were the order of the day. The depositors could not complain because of the rule 'the caveat emptor—buyer beware' that prevailed. Many banks failed due to mismanagement. A key bank in Kerala, Palai Central Bank, was 33 years old and made money by resorting to unconventional business practices. It was now in trouble. The RBI observed it for nine long years, undecided on the action to be taken. There was a great tussle between the management of the bank and the RBI. The tussle went on from 1956 to 1960, with both sides holding their grounds. Iengar played a key role in this as the RBI directed the bank in November 1958 to not declare a dividend until it managed to bring its bad and doubtful debts down to a reasonable level. In June 1960, there was a run on the bank's deposits and the bank collapsed. Finally, in 1960, the RBI caused it to be liquidated as it was finally convinced that the bank had become inherently unstable. This incident caused a run on many banks in Kerala.

This led to the birth of deposit insurance. This was the time when Iengar started canvassing his idea of deposit insurance, which was very stiffly resisted by banks, particularly by larger banks represented by the Indian Banks' Association. Initially, even the government was also not very eager to implement the measure. Undeterred, Iengar kept on pursuing the idea vehemently. Ultimately, the Deposit Insurance Corporation Act was brought into force from 1 January 1962 when the Deposit Insurance Corporation, a wholly owned subsidiary of the RBI, came into existence, two months before Iengar's term as the RBI's governor ended.

It was the failure of the Palai Central Bank that tightened the RBI's grip on commercial banks because the government empowered the RBI to forcibly merge weak banks. It led to a series of mergers and acquisitions in the banking sector and initiated the consolidation of Indian banking. A review of licensing of Indian banks revealed a large number of unlicensed banks. Hence, an active licensing policy was implemented and the unlicensed weak banks were asked either to merge or get liquidated.

In September 1960, the RBI acquired powers to enforce amalgamations and speedier delicensing of banks, which helped give more teeth to its inspections. At the same time, the Bank realized the need to improve inspection machinery after the failure of the Palai Central Bank and Laxmi Bank, where the management was reported to have misappropriated depositors' funds. It was necessary to undertake surprise inspections of banks or even of some of their branches alone and thereby 'detect frauds ... at the appropriate time'.[6] In view of this, in 1961, to reorganize and strengthen its inspection arrangements, the Inspection Department was put under an executive director specially appointed for the purpose. Bank inspections now began to cover many more branches than in the past, and they were also widened to include elements of selective audit. It was also during this period that the Credit Information Bureau was set up to collect and disseminate information on large borrowers among banks.

After the collapse of the Palai Central Bank, Iengar took personal interest in evolving capital adequacy norms for the Indian banks. Like deposit insurance, capital adequacy norms were a radical reform at that point of time. However, Iengar's term ended before this reform could be introduced in the Indian banking sector. Considering the importance deposit insurance and capital adequacy have acquired in modern banking, one realizes how farsighted Iengar was. This measure that required banks to set aside certain percentage of their profits to reserves to augment their capital had its origin in this period.

---

[6]Ibid. 404.

It was in August 1960 that Iengar initiated discussion on the liquidity ratio of Indian banks, which was quite low as compared to international norms. This discussion culminated in the review within the RBI of the existing liquidity provisions in the Banking Companies' Act as well as the RBI Act. The need for higher liquidity ratios was dictated primarily by the need to safeguard the liquidity of the banking system and enable it to withstand the strains of a sudden increase in withdrawals. It led to introduction of mandatory maintenance of CRR and SLR as percentage of deposit liabilities of the banks.

An overall review of the expansion of the RBI's offices took place in 1960. The memorandum submitted by Iengar to the Central Board meeting in December 1960 stated that viewing the long-term requirements, it would plan for expansion of offices in an orderly and integrated manner, so that in the coming years, the Bank's work would increase not only in the traditional lines, namely, the management of note issue, conduct of government business and management of public debt but also in the field of banking operations and control as well as supply of rural and industrial credit. Iengar went on to suggest the establishment of integrated offices at the headquarters (or other principal towns) of the principal states and construction of the RBI's own buildings at these places with a view to acquire the ability to take up additional workload, decentralization of work leading to all-round efficiency, abolition of various note cancellation sections and a reduction in the number of large cross-country remittances.

Iengar, from the outset, was well aware of the possibility that the demands of agricultural credit would require the establishment of specialized institutions for the purpose. When it was suggested to the RBI to suspend banking principles and liberalize lending to the agricultural sector, Iengar had said that it might be better from the country's point of view for a separate corporation to undertake such financing than for the RBI to show many bad debts in its books. As a result of his persistent follow up and efforts, the Agricultural Refinance Corporation Bill, 1962, was introduced in the Lok Sabha in December 1962 and was passed by Parliament in March 1963. Finally, the Agricultural Refinance Corporation opened for business in Bombay on 1 July 1963.

Expanding the cooperative movement was an explicit aspect of the government's programme for rural development in independent India. But it ranked low in its priorities until the mid-1950s. The Planning Commission was dissatisfied with some aspects of existing cooperative policy, in particular the stress on large-sized societies and state governments investing in their share capital. On the other hand, the Bank was convinced that the social objectives of the cooperative movement would not be achieved if the institutions that made up its foundations were not financially viable. Due to the strenuous efforts taken by Iengar, a committee headed by Vaikunth Lal Mehta was formed in 1960 to look into all the aspects of strengthening the cooperative credit movement. In fact, it is Iengar who should be credited for the evolution of primary agricultural societies at village level and District Central Cooperative Banks as the primary source of agricultural credit at district level. Iengar also took special interest in organizing an inspection department for carrying out audit of cooperative banks.

Iengar took painstaking efforts in ensuring that the erstwhile state-associated banks were taken over by the SBI as subsidiaries. In fact, Krishnamachari was keen on annexing these banks to the SBI, even if it had to be done forcefully. Iengar was of the opinion that the process should be smooth and with the consent of the erstwhile princely states that were major shareholders in these banks. He prevailed upon Krishnamachari to explore possibilities of willing cooperation from the managements of these banks in this regard. Ultimately, the shareholders of these banks, notably the Hyderabad State Bank, Bank of Indore, Bank of Patiala, Bank of Travancore, Bank of Bikaner, Bank of Mysore and State Bank of Saurashtra, passed resolutions in their meetings indicating their willingness to be taken over as subsidiaries of the SBI. The SBI (Subsidiary Banks) Bill, 1959 was introduced in Parliament on 4 March 1959, and, after being passed by both the Houses of Parliament, received the assent of the president in September 1959. Thus, the state-associated banks became subsidiaries of the SBI. All these banks have now been merged into the SBI since 2017.

A measure of Iengar's foresight can be found in a speech delivered on February 1962, towards the end of his tenure as the RBI governor. Iengar had identified four areas of potential conflict between the Bank and the central government. These were interest rate policy, deficit financing, cooperative credit policies and management of substandard banks. Two recent governors, Raghuram Rajan and Urjit Patel, left the RBI due to differences with the government on one or other of the above four issues.

TRIVIA

1. In the 87 years since its formation, the RBI has never had a female governor. There have, however, been several women who served as deputy governors: Usha Thorat, Shyamala Gopinath and Kishori Jayendra Udeshi, among others. Their tenures were noteworthy for their contribution to the development of the institution.
2. S. Jagannathan and M. Narasimham joined the World Bank and the IMF, respectively, as India's representatives after relinquishing the post of governor, while L.K. Jha, R.N. Malhotra, Bimal Jalan, Y.V. Reddy and Raghuram Rajan joined the RBI as governors after their stint at the IMF or the World Bank.
3. D. Subbarao stood first in the all-India Civil Service Examination for entry into the Indian Administrative Service (IAS) and Indian Foreign Service in 1972. He was one of the

first people from the Indian Institute of Technology (IIT) to join the ICS.

4. L.K. Jha is the only governor to have shifted to the USA as India's ambassador after his two-year stint as the RBI governor.
5. Of the 25 governors so far, only nine have served a term of five years or more. Of these nine, only three served a term of exactly five years each.
6. Both H.V.R. Iengar and P.C. Bhattacharya came to the RBI as governors after a stint as chairmen of the SBI. Iengar was from the ICS while Bhattacharyya belonged to the Indian Audit and Accounts Service.

7

P.C. Bhattacharya

Paresh Chandra Bhattacharya was the seventh governor of the RBI from 1 March 1962 to 30 June 1967. He was a member of the Indian Audits and Accounts Service and served as the expenditure secretary to the Ministry of Finance before replacing H.V.R. Iengar as the chairman of the SBI in 1957. In 1962, he took over from Iengar as governor of the RBI, and his first few months in office were a continuation of Iengar's policy efforts to consolidate rather than expand. Bhattacharya kept to himself and was modest by temperament but firm when it mattered. He worked under three finance ministers: Morarji Desai, T.T. Krishnamachari and Sachindra Chaudhuri. Unlike some of his predecessors, he shared a good working relationship with all of them.

After the 1962 elections, Desai and Bhattacharya took a tough stand against the states' rising overdrafts. Desai was concerned about the diversion of plan resources, which resulted from states' overdrafts and the central government's manner of covering them. He informed the chief ministers that he had authorized the RBI to stop payments issued by states where overdrafts were not cleared after the agreed notice period of one month. Bhattacharya was reluctant to take so drastic a step. He was worried that the Centre could not wash its hands of the problem, since if a state's payments were stopped, Delhi might have to take over its financial administration. Desai, on the other hand, wanted to underline the importance of making state governments 'realise that overdrafts from the Reserve Bank are not to be used for meeting ... ways and means difficulties'.[1] In fact, a notice was issued to the government of Bihar in 1963 stating that their payments would be stopped if overdrafts were not cleared in 30 days. The Bihar government asked for two months to clear the overdraft, which it managed to do, and the crisis was averted. Unfortunately, however, Desai and Bhattacharya's efforts to instil financial discipline in states were in vain. The issue of overdrafts kept haunting the RBI. Bhattacharya continued to try and discipline the states in the matter of overdrafts throughout his tenure with little success.

A strong rural credit structure was essential for boosting agricultural production. However, the country's hopes of setting up a viable and inexpensive credit system for agriculturalists, in the form of cooperative credit mechanism, remained weak and ineffective at most places. In March 1964, an informal group was constituted to review institutional arrangements in the field of agricultural credit. Bhattacharya chaired the group, and its report was submitted in January 1965. It affirmed that the three-tier cooperative credit structure was the most suitable means of dispensing agricultural credit in Indian conditions. According to the group, the cooperative credit policies adopted were generally adequate, but they were not always fully implemented. The group suggested strengthening the cooperative credit structure in the country in order to dispense agricultural credit, while also forming agriculture credit corporations to augment the efforts of the cooperative credit institutions as a temporary measure. Soon, the Agricultural Credit Corporation Bill was passed in Parliament and it became an Act in December 1968, although Bhattacharya had left office by that time.

---

[11]Balachandran, G., *The Reserve Bank of India: 1951–1967*, Mumbai, Oxford University Press, 1998, p. 200.

Bhattacharya envisaged that the impact of cooperative credit institutions on the monetary and credit situation would become increasingly significant over time. He, therefore, felt it was necessary to bring cooperative banking institutions within the ambit of the RBI's control, and to give the RBI powers over cooperative banks analogous to those it enjoyed over joint stock banks. Bhattacharya also stressed the need to extend deposit insurance to these banks so as to strengthen their operations. The Banking Laws (Application to Cooperative Societies) Bill was passed by Parliament and became an Act in September 1965, extending the RBI's powers over cooperative banks.

Bhattacharya took the initiative to make the RBI consider stipulating ceilings on the individual and group exposures of banks. For this purpose, an amendment to Section 21 of the Act was proposed, authorizing the RBI to stipulate the maximum amount of advances or other financial accommodation and guarantees that a bank could make to an individual, firm, association of persons or a company. The RBI board insisted that the RBI should exercise its powers to give directions to banks about the maximum financial accommodation they could give to any single borrower only after it was satisfied that it was 'desirable to do so in the interests of the depositors'.[2] For its part, the government canvassed these provisions of the Bill vigorously in Parliament as a part of its efforts to free commercial banks from the influence of big business. In fact, while the Bill was being debated in Parliament, some members of the Congress demanded the nationalization of commercial banks in the country (which ultimately happened in 1969, during Indira Gandhi's leadership). The Bill was passed and became an Act in December 1963.

It was Bhattacharya who had advocated to bankers in 1964 that the time had come to 'give fuller play' to the rate of interest

[2]Ibid. 431.

'as a device to attract more funds into the system'. He cautioned the banks that loans from the RBI were available only to 'tide over temporary difficulties' and that they could not look at RBI as a source of funding all through the year.[3] He nudged the banks to increase interest rates on deposits to attract more funds so as to be able to fund the industry. The term 'structure of deposit rates', Bhattacharya argued, should be such that it induces a larger flow of genuine savings or idle balances into banks in the form of time deposits. In fact, since the rate of interest became an important tool to manipulate the flow of deposits in the banking system, the RBI decided in September 1964 to prescribe maximum interest rates on shorter-term deposits and indicate minimum interest rates on longer-term deposits. Apart from rationalizing the deposit-rate structure to enable the banking system to mobilize savings better and thereby help fulfil one of the objectives of the Bank's credit policy, the object of the exercise was also to encourage banks to reduce their dependence upon the RBI for accommodation.[4]

In the 1963–64 Budget, Desai declared the government's intention to set up an investment trust that would afford the common man 'a means to acquire a share in the widening prosperity based on steady industrial growth', that combined 'security and a reasonable return'.[5] The task of preparing the blueprint of the trust was entrusted to the RBI. The Unit Trust of India (UTI) Act was passed in December 1963 and the UTI came into being on 1 February 1964 as an offshoot of the RBI.

Although the IFCI was the central lending agency for industrial finance, its performance was below par, as it was constrained due to severe lacunae in its legislation. Krishnamachari was, therefore, keen on a more proactive financing agency for industrial finance. He asked Bhattacharya to work on it, and the governor submitted

[3]Ibid. 122.
[4]Ibid. 121–3.
[5]Ibid. 542.

the outline of the DFIs to the finance minister in November 1963. According to this guideline, the 'general conception of the new institution' was that it should be able to take a 'coordinated view of the problem of industrial finance in all its aspects in the context of planned industrial development'.[6] Bhattacharya named the development bank 'Industrial Development Bank of India'. The IDBI came into existence on 1 July 1964 after the necessary legislation was passed in Parliament as a subsidiary owned wholly by the RBI, and began working as the apex financial institution for industry.

Bhattacharya's tenure saw a major uproar erupt in Parliament and the media when the rupee was devalued by a huge 36.5 per cent in June 1966. The decision had actually been taken by Indira Gandhi in March that year when she visited the USA and met the representatives of the World Bank and IMF, but it was kept a well-guarded secret. Even the finance minister did not know. Senior officials such as Bhattacharya, L.K. Jha and I.G. Patel had been involved in negotiations with the World Bank and IMF for close to two years. India was in desperate need of external aid since the country's foreign-exchange reserves had been dwindling continuously due to poor planning, the wars of 1962 and 1965 and a severe drought. One of the major conditions of the World Bank and IMF for extending aid was the devaluation of the rupee. Having explored all available options, the officials had come to the conclusion that there was no alternative other than devaluing the rupee. Unfortunately, the country could not make the best use of this measure.

Following the devaluation in June 1966, the governor was the chief spokesperson of the view that devaluation by itself was not a solution. In one of his addresses, he said that 'it was a challenge to stand on our feet' and went on to state: 'The success

[6]Ibid. 536.

with which we are able to contain inflation, increase exports and reduce dependence on others for imports will determine how soon we could make a turnaround in our balance of payments.'[7] These thoughts were indicative of the fact that the governor was aware of the conditions in which the country could hope to maintain the devalued rupee rate. Inflation had to be kept firmly in check if the maintenance of any export advantage derived from devaluation could be translated into a gain in reserves.

So, in crafting a package of supportive measures, Bhattacharya took special care to see that there was no general relaxation of the credit policy; in fact, there was an overall tightening of credit expansion in the interest of monetary stability, even while ensuring its flow to various sectors according to their priorities. He was constantly chiding the finance minister against the continually expanding deficits of the central and state governments and advised greater restraint in government expenditure. The policy issue that came to the fore was: Could the decision to devalue have been avoided? A ministry note to members of Parliament explained why the decision had to be taken. The note clearly stated:

> The action could not be postponed as all further aid negotiations hinged on it. It is extremely doubtful whether, without demonstrable evidence of our determination to push up our exports and improve the internal viability of our economy, we shall continue to get external credits, particularly, as we are already at the stage when we have to incur fresh debts in order to pay off old ones. Without reasonable prospects of aid forthcoming on the scale contemplated by us, the finalisation of the Fourth Plan will be still further postponed.[8]

[7] *The Reserve Bank of India: Volume 3, 1967–1981*, Mumbai, Central Office, Reserve Bank of India, 2005, p. 520.
[8] Balachandran, G., *The Reserve Bank of India: 1951–1967*, Mumbai, Oxford University Press, 1998, pp. 672–90.

As governor of the RBI, Bhattacharya strongly opposed the nationalization of private banks in India, writing a letter to then Deputy Prime Minister Morarji Desai, warning him about the costs of nationalizing the banks and saying that it was not desirable. During his tenure, the size of the currency notes of denomination five, 10 and 100 were reduced in size for economic reasons. Bhattacharya's tenure coincided with the pursuit of a more active monetary policy. He was instrumental in the introduction of the Credit Authorisation Scheme (CAS) as an instrument of credit regulation.

Based on the experience gained in the second and third Five-Year Plans and closer scrutiny of the estimates for the fourth Five-Year Plan, the RBI under Bhattacharya realized that the proposed plan size needed to be curtailed in view of the available resources. Therefore, it proposed to the government that the plan should be based on 'more realistic estimates of both domestic and foreign resources' and that a smaller plan was needed 'if we are really serious about [avoiding] deficit financing'.[9] In April 1967, Bhattacharya wrote to Desai stating that the estimates would undergo changes if the financial resources actually available for the central government's plan expenditures fell short of earlier estimates. He suggested that the plan be 'reworked in light of the new situation and after making realistic estimates of the possibilities in regard to overall income growth, scope for modifying the existing savings-income ratios, trends in foreign trade and payments, etc'.[10]

Similar advice had been tendered by then Governor Rau to Pandit Nehru at the end of the first Five-Year Plan, suggesting that the second Five-Year Plan be curtailed in size to fit the available resources. Rau had been brushed aside by Nehru, and India had paid the price in the years that followed.

---

[9]Ibid. 24.
[10]Ibid.

Bhattacharya, having known Rau's fate and having understood the nature of the government–RBI relationship, was not unduly bothered about the autonomy and independence of the RBI vis-à-vis the government. He shared a good personal rapport with both Desai and Krishnamachari. He also played a major role in piloting the country's external economic diplomacy during his last two years in office. The RBI, under Bhattacharya, started dealing with the finance ministry more at the level of its civil servants than directly at the political level, and this trend continued thereafter. To a certain extent, this amounted to a diminution in the Bank's standing and influence and a significant reduction in its access to the corridors of political power. It also meant a greater formalization of its links with the finance ministry. So tremendous was his clout in the corridors of power that it was rumoured that Sachindra Chaudhuri, who took over as finance minister after Krishnamachari, who had resigned in December 1965, had been the governor's nominee for the crucial Cabinet position.[11]

Bhattacharya and Krishnamachari were close. The former was with the SBI during the latter's earlier stint as finance minister, and the two men weathered the storm of the Haridas Mundra scam together. By quirk of circumstances, Krishnamachari returned to the Ministry of Finance in August 1963 and set about to hasten the implementation of his ideas of institutional development that were left unfinished in his first stint as finance minister. The RBI, under Bhattacharya's leadership, effectively complemented Krishnamachari's initiative to set up institutions such as the IDBI and the UTI. The complementary roles they played in guiding institutional and developmental initiatives and financing programmes to materialize during these years helped the RBI and the finance ministry establish a close working relationship. It is apparent from the RBI's records that the governor and the

[11]Ibid. 734.

deputy governors regularly advised the government on a variety of issues, including some in which the RBI could have little interest in any capacity.[12]

However, Bhattacharya did try to translate his newfound influence in the corridors of power into a measure of autonomy for the RBI. This was evident in changes to the bank rate four times between 1963 and 1965, when the bank rate had otherwise been stagnant since 1957. In fact, Krishnamachari was reported to have made efforts to claim the prerogative to announce bank rate changes in 1964–65. Bhattacharya saw in Krishnamachari's suggestion an effort to usurp an important responsibility of the RBI. Contrary to expectations, he showed that he was made of sterner stuff and refused stridently to yield to the minister on this issue. He is reported to have insisted on retaining the RBI's right of precedence in announcing the bank rate. Although this was arguably of only symbolic importance, the bank rate policy showed that the RBI had come into its own.

It was Bhattacharya's initiative that saw the creation of the Department of Banking Operations and Development (DBOD) in 1965 by merging the DBD and DBO, a move that was long overdue. Bhattacharya's other important accomplishment was the formation of a separate department of non-banking companies in March 1966. Another area where he left his imprint was in the creation of the secretary's department, by upgrading the secretary's section that dealt with not only the work relating to meetings of the Central Board and its committees but also the work associated with the government's public borrowings and the management of public debt.

---

[12]Ibid. 712.

TRIVIA

1. Sir James Braid Taylor is so far the youngest to join the RBI as governor, although Sir C.D. Deshmukh, Manmohan Singh and Raghuram Rajan had also become governors of the RBI at a young age, that is, below 50.
2. Urjit Patel is the only RBI governor of Indian origin who was born and raised outside India. Patel grew up in Kenya and became an Indian citizen only after joining the RBI.
3. For 78 years between 1935 and 2013, every single governor except C. Rangarajan had come from within the government system. Rangarajan was a well-known professor of economics at prestigious institutes, such as the Indian Institute of Management Ahmedabad (IIMA), India, and the University of Pennsylvania, USA, before being appointed as the deputy governor of the RBI in 1982. Another noteworthy exception was Raghuram Rajan, who was the president of the American Finance Association in 2011 and was picked as the chief economic advisor to the Government of India. He worked as such until 4 September 2013, when he was nominated as the RBI governor.
4. The following governors had served the RBI as deputy governors before they were elevated to governorship: Sir James Taylor, Sir C.D. Deshmukh, K.G. Ambegaokar, Amitav Ghosh, C. Rangarajan, Y.V. Reddy and Urjit Patel.

8

L.K. Jha

Lakshmi Kant Jha was a multifaceted and versatile personality who excelled in several walks of life. He was an eminent economist, a distinguished administrator, an able diplomat and a sage counsellor with great expertise and mature judgement. Jha was the governor of the RBI from 1 July 1967 to 3 May 1970, at a time when the Indian economy was going through one of its most difficult phases. The country was shaken by food scarcity and the concerns resulted in the much-celebrated initiative of Green Revolution. Jha, through his leadership, was able to make the RBI an influential force in shaping such initiatives. Due to the overall situation of scarcity, the poor in the country were severely distressed. As such, poverty reduction became main focus of all policies. The RBI under Jha's stewardship contributed to designing and implementing many such anti-poverty policies.

Popularly known as L.K., Lakshmi Kant Jha was born in Bihar on 22 November 1913. He graduated from Banaras Hindu University, Varanasi, and Trinity College, Cambridge, UK. At Trinity College, he was a student of renowned economists like Arthur Cecil Pigou, John Maynard Keynes, Harold Laski and Sir Dennis Holme Robertson. He joined the ICS in 1936. After serving in Bihar in the districts and in the Provincial Secretariat, he was endorsed to the Government of India in 1942. There he worked successively as the deputy secretary to the Department of Food and Civil Supplies, chief controller of imports and exports, joint secretary to the Ministry of Commerce and Industry and secretary to the Ministry of Heavy Industry. Having impressed the powers that be as India's principal representative at the meetings of the General Agreement on Tariffs and Trade and as its chairman in 1957–58, he became secretary to the Department of Economic Affairs, Ministry of Finance, in 1960. Later on, he was appointed to the newly created post of principal secretary to then Prime Minister Lal Bahadur Shastri in 1964. Subsequently, he continued in the same capacity even under Prime Minister Indira Gandhi.

Jha was by far one of the most distinguished and accomplished civil servants to occupy the office of the governor and was responsible for giving a distinct development orientation to the RBI policies. The RBI, under his leadership, was an influential force in shaping landmark policies for the devaluation of rupee, the Green Revolution, social control followed by nationalization of 14 major commercial banks and so on. The social controls over commercial banks were introduced as an experiment in 1968, as a part of which the National Credit Council was established. However, Indira Gandhi felt that this would not serve the purpose and, as a result, the decision to nationalize banks was taken. Among other developments, gold controls were brought on a statutory basis, deposit insurance was, in principle, extended to cooperative banks, the lead bank scheme was introduced to facilitate credit delivery and the Agricultural Credit Board was set up.

The problem of rural credit has always remained one of the most complex issues in India. After Independence, not only did rural credit become a political imperative with 90 per cent of India's population living in villages, it also became a strong economic need because 60 per cent of the GDP came from agriculture. But the challenges of expanding rural credit were so great in the mid-1960s that the RBI had been frustrated. The thought that it should force commercial banks to go rural had started gaining ground. Social control of banks versus outright nationalization was a subject that was raging in those days in corridors of power in the wake of the two droughts of 1965 and 1966. It was during this challenging time that, in 1967, the highly respected and shrewd L.K. Jha took over as the governor of the RBI.

Jha was an advocate of social control of banks but was opposed to nationalization, although he never articulated his views expressly. He was not an undiscerning friend of the private-sector banks. He was aware that they had utterly and completely failed to spread banking to rural areas, which was the need of the hour. In 1961, there were only 5,100 branches, of which over 99 per cent were in urban areas. At a meeting of bankers in 1967, a frustrated Jha said that he was all for slowing down branch expansion in urban areas. The bankers were complaining to him that they were being discriminated against compared to the foreign banks since foreign banks were allowed to do business in metro cities while Indian banks were being asked to open branches in rural areas. The foreign banks, on the other hand, were saying that it was they who were being discriminated against because they felt they were not being allowed to open more branches. The heated discussion went on for three years before Jha settled the debate by pointing out, first, that foreign banks helped raise foreign exchange and, second, that compared to Indian banks, number of branches allowed to be opened by foreign banks were miniscule.[1]

The nationalization of major Indian banks in 1969 remains one of the most important chapters in the banking history of the country. Indira Gandhi's hesitant debut lasted for three-and-a-half years, which resulted in a political drift in the country. Many in

[1]Srinivasa Raghavan, T.C.A., *A Crown of Thorns: The Governors of the RBI*, Chennai, Westland, 2016, p. 19.

her camp advised her to nationalize banks and end the political impasse. Finally, in a sudden and unprecedented move, she nationalized 14 banks in 1969. According to sources, Gandhi did not consult Jha, knowing fully well that he was a strong advocate of social control and was not in favour of nationalization. When Gandhi called Jha to come over to New Delhi on 17 July, he went with a comprehensive note in support of social control. She is reported to have told him that he could keep the note he was carrying on her table and go to the next room and help in drafting the legislation on nationalization of banks. Gandhi also asked D.N. Ghosh, deputy secretary to the finance ministry, to draft the legislation with the help of R.K. Seshadri, executive director of the RBI, who had experience in preparing draft legislation.[2]

The entire work of drafting was done in the RBI building in Delhi and was overseen by Jha. Gandhi informed I.G. Patel, the secretary to the Department of Economic Affairs, that she had taken the decision to nationalize banks on *political considerations* and asked him to prepare her speech to be delivered on 19 July when she declared the Banking Companies (Acquisition and Transfer of Undertakings) Ordinance, taking over the undertaking of 14 commercial banks having deposits not less than ₹50 crore as of June 1969. It was at the instance of Jha that the separate identities of the 14 banks were preserved. Even otherwise, creation of a monolithic institution was not considered appropriate considering the past experience of LIC. The decision to maintain separate identities of the 14 banks was welcomed by the experts and luminaries like Nani Palkhiwala hoping that it would spur competition and better services to customers. As recounted by Jha himself, the international reaction to nationalization of banks was quite passive since the success of Green Revolution had overshadowed all other news.

[2]Ibid. 20.

The nationalization of 14 major banks without taking the RBI into confidence created further difficulties for monetary policy as the RBI's autonomy was abridged even further because of what may be termed as fiscal dominance. Polity moved from party to person and economy moved from private to State. It was ironical that Jha, who was considered a great economic liberal, was called upon to oversee this process in the banking industry. In the days to come, the RBI was consulted but only for the sake of it; its views were not necessarily considered in policy-making. Even the autonomy the RBI enjoyed, as far as fixation of bank rate was concerned, was lost due to high degree of activism shown by the Ministry of Finance and the Planning Commission. Such was the jolt felt in the RBI that when its board met a few days after the nationalization, no records were kept of the discussion. The whole meeting was described in a single line as a brief discussion on the implications of the bank nationalization ordinance.

What was most disturbing for the RBI was the impression that was created in the media that it was opposed to nationalization. In fact, as vice-chairman of the National Credit Council, Jha had ensured that a large number of documents were submitted on different aspects of social control. The Bank gave substantial inputs to the work of the groups formed by the National Credit Council, helped to provide the secretariat for the Council and assisted in creation of a cell attached to the Banking Commission. These actions by themselves did not imply that Jha was opposed to nationalization of major Indian banks since it was all being done as per the desires of the political bosses. All the oral accounts state that although Jha did not favour bank nationalization, he refrained from articulating his personal views on the subject.

Jha convened a meeting of the custodians of the 14 nationalized banks and the chairman of the SBI in Bombay in 1969 to chalk out the immediate steps necessary to implement the objectives of nationalization. He discussed the responsibilities of the public-sector banks in the new scenario and ways to achieve better distribution of credit as well as improvements in banking services and profitability. He advised the banks to not compete among themselves as regards rate of interest chargeable on advances and give favourable treatment to small loans.

As a follow-up to nationalization, a scheme of guarantees for lending by banks to channelize more funds to the priority sectors and other sectors that had remained neglected was launched, which resulted in setting up of the Credit Guarantee Corporation of India under the aegis of the RBI. During this period, the RBI conceptualized priority-sector lending. Considering the political and social demands for apportionment of credit to priority sectors, the RBI prescribed priority-sector lending targets to be achieved by the banks in a given time frame. This practice of targeted lending continues even today, with enhanced scope.

Two gentlemen had challenged the constitutional validity of the ordinance issued to take over 14 major commercial banks in the Supreme Court. In February 1970, a full bench of the Supreme Court upheld the constitutional validity of the ordinance and the right of Parliament to enact a law regarding banking. After the legal tangle over nationalization was sorted out in March 1970, in a conference with the heads of DBOD from various centres, Jha articulated the changing role of the RBI with the message:

> The Bank's main duty was to ensure the flow of adequate credit to the neglected sectors of the economy in the country, and not only to look to the safety aspect of funds but also to see that the funds were not lent to a borrower who was likely to misuse the credit by diverting it for speculative or other purposes. He also said that inspectors could play

a vital role in ensuring that the declared policies of the government were implemented.[3]

Consequently, four types of inspections were decided upon: (i) inspection to assess the financial position; (ii) centre-wise inspection of branches; (iii) ad hoc inspections to examine implementation of selective credit controls, frauds, complaints, etc., and (iv) inspection to examine the systems and performance of banks. Till date, there is not much change in the inspection criteria except that inspection has now been replaced by risk-based supervision.[4]

During this period, the limit of deposits to be covered under deposit insurance was raised from ₹1,500 to ₹5,000, with effect from 1 January 1968. The significant increase in the coverage of insured deposits instilled public confidence in the banking system, augmented deposits and fostered banking in unbanked areas.

As a consequence of reduced external aid in 1968–69, economic planning in the country suffered. Long-term planning was suspended, and three annual plans were executed to consolidate short-run gains. At this point, in a personal communication with Professor D.R. Gadgil, deputy chairman of the Planning Commission, articulating his views on approach to planning, Jha warned that rigid plan targets with high growth rates could result in frustration since achievements are forgotten and only shortfalls are highlighted. His other pragmatic suggestion was that the aid requirements should not be seen as an index of dependence but as a measure of what can be achieved if the nature and quantum of external support were adequate. He stressed that aid-giving countries find it very difficult, economically and politically, to refinance past loans than to sanction new ones.

---

[3]*The Reserve Bank of India: Volume 3, 1967–1981*, Mumbai, Central Office, Reserve Bank of India, 2005, p. 223.

[4]Ibid.

He further suggested that reliance on foreign capital, whether official or private, should be reduced to the minimum and only limited amount of foreign investment should be accepted only for projects deemed as important.

Jha was an ardent supporter of liberalization, a process that has gained momentum since his time. He was of the view that although liberalization may temporarily bring adverse terms of trade in its wake, in the long run, it would lead to increase in exports and greater competitiveness in the economy. He was not pleased with the way control was administered in the Exchange Control Department and insisted that the control be simplified. He was particularly keen to simplify the foreign-exchange regulations that impinged on individuals. He was of the view that the RBI was designed to deal with corporations, especially banks, but, in reality, was spending a high percentage of its time in dealing with individual cases involving petty amounts, resulting in delays in dealing with important cases involving large sums of foreign exchange. As a result, the government decided to delegate the maximum possible powers to authorized dealers to deal with such requests on their own. As per Jha's thinking, the RBI needed to move towards a new pattern of responsibilities, in which it was seen as an essential link between the interests of business and the demands of officialdom.

He played a crucial role in shaping the country's economic policies for nearly four decades. With his fine blend of theory, practice and rare pragmatism, he had an instinctive feel for policies that could work in the Indian context. At the same time, he conceptualized and articulated forward-looking policies for dynamic growth of the Indian economy. He had a significant role in shaping the Industrial Policy Resolution of 1956, which made the concept of mixed economy operational and provided stimulus for the country's industrial development. Furthermore, as the chairman of the Indirect Taxation Enquiry Committee, he made numerous valuable and enduring contributions to the improvement of India's fiscal system.

Jha effectively pleaded the cause of India and other developing countries in many international fora and was a highly respected member of the Brandt Commission that advocated a new world economic order, in which the developing countries would have a more equitable share. As the chairman of the Economic Administration Reforms Commission, he was responsible for changing the direction of economic policy towards controlled deregulation as a preliminary step to full liberalization. Jha was also one of the most active officials responsible for the major overhaul of the Foreign Exchange Regulation Act (FERA) 1947, which gave way to FERA, 1973.

Jha sometimes faced criticism from the press, evidence of which can be found in a critical editorial titled 'Half-Way House', in which the *Economic Times*, on 2 August 1967, acidly commented on the increasing budget deficit, and further said that 'The Bank lacks the necessary courage. Its policy will remain timid so long as it remains an appendage of the Finance Ministry and so long as it refuses to recognise that it is an independent central banking authority.'[5]

After his tenure at the RBI ended in 1970, Jha served as India's ambassador to the USA and as governor of Jammu and Kashmir. When the Bangladesh Liberation War broke out in 1971, he effectively presented the Indian viewpoint to world forums. He was also a member of the widely acclaimed Brandt Commission that made a persuasive case for North–South cooperation. Global cooperation, which is now so much a part of our daily discourse, draws its intellectual origins from the Brandt Commission Report of the 1970s to which Jha had contributed handsomely. At the time of his death on 16 January 1988, he was a member of the Rajya Sabha.

[5]Ibid. 354.

9

B.N. Adarkar

Bhaskar Namdeo Adarkar joined the RBI as deputy governor on 16 June 1965 for a term of five years. He was the interim governor of the RBI for 42 days, from 4 May 1970 to 15 June 1970.

Unlike his predecessors who were from the ICS, Adarkar was an economist and had served in the Office of the Economic Adviser of the Government of India. He had held various important positions in the Ministry of Commerce and Industry. In March 1947, he was appointed by the Government of India to create a health insurance scheme for industrial workers. A year later, the report he submitted became the basis for the Employees' State Insurance Act of 1948 that highlighted the need to safeguard the Indian employees from contingencies like illness, physical disablement and death that take place as workplace hazards, ultimately impacting their earning capacity.

When Finance Minister Yashwantrao Chavan expressed serious concern on fraud in the banking sector, Adarkar, then governor of the RBI, wrote to the Ministry of Finance:

> The internal working of commercial banks in India has so many deficiencies that it is a matter of surprise that the number of frauds actually occurring is so small. Over the last few years, we have been trying to improve the working

> in many respects, but this is a task which will take some years to be fully accomplished. My four years of hard work in the DBOD were not enough. There are a number of areas where it is essential to improve our inspection procedures and also bring about radical changes in the internal working of banks.... I would ask you to appreciate that given the limitations of personnel and the importance and urgency of developing the social aspects of banking, the Reserve Bank could not possibly do all it wished by way of cleaning up the internal working of banks. In fact, it was the Reserve Bank's excessive preoccupation with mere policing that had led to the development work being somewhat neglected prior to the introduction of social control. I recognise, however, that both development and improvement of personnel and procedures must now be pursued simultaneously and with equal vigour.[1]

In April 1970, controversy followed after a fraud of significant amount of foreign exchange was detected at the London branch of the Central Bank of India, which had not been inspected by the RBI since 1960. Adarkar explained that inspecting overseas branches was expensive and it had been decided in 1960 to undertake inspections of foreign branches once in three years. Furthermore, branches in Asia and Africa were given priority. Branches of banks like the Central Bank of India, which had large networks overseas, were supposed to be inspected by senior officers. The RBI had been unable to spare any senior officers in the execution of social control initiatives and the merger of smaller banks, and the inspections had fallen to the wayside. After strenuous efforts to recover the money and protracted litigation, the Central Bank of India managed to partially recover the money

[1] *The Reserve Bank of India: Volume 3, 1967–1981*, Mumbai, Central Office, Reserve Bank of India, 2005, p. 224.

lost in the fraud. The bank management was found to have ignored the RBI's periodic warnings in favour of lassitude.[2]

Adarkar's signature appears on the two-, five-, 10- and 100-rupee notes commemorating the birth centenary of Mahatma Gandhi, issued in August 1970. Due to his short tenure, his signature does not appear on any other rupee notes.

[2]Ibid. 256–61.

10

S. Jagannathan

Sarukkai Jagannathan, the tenth governor of the RBI who served from 16 June 1970 to 19 May 1975, was India's executive director at the World Bank before taking up the governorship of the RBI. Interestingly, he relinquished office at the RBI to take up the post of India's executive director at the IMF.

Jagannathan's predecessor Jha was a towering personality and his departure from the RBI turned out to be the beginning of a period of growing influence of the Ministry of Finance and diminishing stature of the RBI. The people in the government felt that the RBI did not understand aspirations of the people or compulsions of the government. The RBI was seen as too conservative and Jagannathan was expected to be 'accommodating'. This did turn out to be the case, and the erosion of authority of the RBI that began in this period continued for over the next decade and a half.

Contrary to general belief, there were skirmishes with the Ministry of Finance in the initial period of his tenure. On the government's directives, banks had planned a branch expansion programme that the RBI deemed ambitious. Some of the lead banks lagged behind in this respect, which was termed by the Finance Minister Y.B. Chavan as unsatisfactory performance of some lead banks. The government was also concerned by the falling ratio of rural and semi-urban branches in the overall branch-expansion programme. However, Jagannathan, whose sympathies were with commercial banks, defended them, saying that the overall direction and pace of branch expansion had been reasonably satisfactory, while the individual performance of a few banks had not been up to the mark.[1]

Certain exemptions from applicability of the CAS were granted in May 1969, with respect to advances of state electricity boards and public-sector enterprises as well as advances granted against guarantees of central and state governments. These exemptions came to be reviewed during 1971. It was thought that projects that had been approved by the Planning Commission should primarily be financed by the central or state governments from their resources. Other suitable projects could be financed by the IDBI and other term-lending institutions, if the need arose. However, there was no justifiable reason for commercial banks to lend to these projects. Although the thinking was very timely, it was not pursued considering the elections were around the corner. It took almost three years for the changes to be made applicable from March 1973 in view of increasing demand for funds from state electricity boards.

Chavan expressed his great displeasure at the growing frauds in the public-sector banks. On 25 June 1971, he wrote to Jagannathan:

> I have been very much perturbed over the spate of frauds in recent weeks in some of the public sector banks. You will agree that what is at stake in these bank frauds is not merely the large sums of money involved, but also the reputation and the image of public sector banks in general and the trust and confidence reposed by the public in the banking system of the country.[2]

---

[1]*The Reserve Bank of India: Volume 3, 1967–1981*, Mumbai, Central Office, Reserve Bank of India, 2005, p. 68.

[2]Ibid. 224.

He wanted the RBI to undertake a detailed study to understand deficiencies in the public-sector banks and remedial measures to eliminate the risk of frauds. Accordingly, centre-wise inspection of branches was initiated briskly. Study teams were deputed as to how the inspections could be made more effective. The teams suggested certain important changes in the way inspection of branches were being carried out, so as to save almost 44 per cent of the time that was being spent on inspections and, in turn, making it more effective.

The government approach towards allowing banks to open branches abroad was quite rigid while the RBI's approach in this regard was quite flexible. The RBI under Jagannathan was of the view that unless banks opened branches abroad, they would never acquire the necessary competence in international finance. It was of the opinion that getting a licence or its equivalent from a foreign monetary authority depended not so much upon a bank having or not having a foreign branch already but upon its credit standing, its size and management. Chavan had indicated to the governor in April 1975 that, as a rule, it would be desirable for the government to accept and act on the recommendations of the RBI. He agreed to pass on to the RBI any facts and suggestions that would enable it to consider and take a final decision on the matter. However, this turned out to be a great illusion as, in May 1975, the government decided to make the Ministry of Finance the focal point for dealing with applications for opening branches abroad, thereby curtailing the role of the RBI in this regard.

The IDBI had been incorporated as a fully owned subsidiary of the RBI in 1964. However, since the government considered the RBI to be too conservative, there was a proposal to delink the IDBI from the RBI in 1973. The idea was that the delinking would give the government control over long-term funds and the capital market. It had already gained control over the short-term funds by nationalizing the 14 public-sector banks. Jagannathan was fiercely opposed to the delinking. Despite the RBI's opposition, legislation in the form of the Public Financial Institutions Law (Amendment) Bill was introduced in the Lok Sabha on 22 December 1973, considered as a retrograde piece of legislation by some of the members of the JPC that was set up to go into the details of the proposal. The All India Reserve Bank Employees Association was also opposed to the legislation. However, the Bill was passed and the IDBI was delinked from the RBI from 16 February 1976 and its control was taken over by the finance ministry. The UTI was also delinked from the RBI at the same time.

It appears that Jagannathan was not able to maintain the autonomy of the RBI vis-à-vis the Ministry of Finance that continued to impose its authority on the RBI in various subtle ways. It informed the RBI on 11 November 1974 of its acceptance of the Estimates Committee's recommendation of a minimum of 33.3 per cent of lending to the priority sector and sent letters to that effect directly to the chief executives of public-sector banks. Ordinarily, the RBI should have been asked to send these letters. The RBI should have protested this encroachment of its authority and being sidelined while dealing with the commercial banks. However, it did not appear to have protested on this encroachment of its turf. Instead, the RBI followed the government's directive with its own advisory to keep up the pretense of giving directions to banks on matters relating to monetary and credit policies.

Jagannathan's tenure of office was characterized by a very active monetary policy in the wake of unprecedented inflation in the country following the oil shock; an exponential expansion of banking offices in pursuance of one of the important objectives of nationalization; the establishment of Credit Guarantee Corporation of India; the setting up of State Level Bankers' Committees and the shift to floating rates regime. Indian rupee notes of denominations of 20 and 50 were introduced, and these bore his signature.

An interesting episode that relates to the non-availability of good quality currency notes in those days is worth narrating. In 1973, the availability of good currency notes in circulation had become precarious. The supplies from the currency presses were dwindling as the paper supply from Security Paper Mill, Hoshangabad, was irregular and not enough. The supply position of currency notes from the presses did not improve in the coming months and eventually the situation became so dire that Jagannathan had to address a letter directly to Chavan, pointing out that the problems faced were more important and critical than apparent at first glance. The government was directly in charge of the production of currency note paper at Hoshangabad and the printing of currency notes at Nashik, whereas the RBI was responsible for the issue of currency, the withdrawal of soiled notes and their replacement with new notes. So, naturally in public eyes, the RBI was seen as the office concerned with currency notes. The fall in the level of production of currency note paper at Hoshangabad had aggravated the situation. To drive home the point, Jagannathan enclosed a letter he had received from a disgruntled member of the public. The letter read as follows:

> The Reserve Bank Governor
>
> Bombay-1
>
> Damn You!
>
> You and your officers deserve to be shot dead for your bungling. For our convenience, we bank our money in nearby banks. They give me soiled and torn notes. They say the money has been got from Reserve Bank. So, they won't give good notes. If we go to shop or hotel, we cannot exchange the notes for our necessities. What the hell do you want me to do with the notes? Neither the bank which gave me would accept them nor shopkeepers. So, we have to come

> all the way to your stupid office and wait in queue? Why the hell can't you withdraw old notes at source itself, i.e., in your office itself. For your mismanagement, you should be given a garland of torn notes.
>
> Sd: N. Akhileshwar[3]

He then reiterated some of the important recommendations made in the past by the RBI, such as import of currency note paper, minting of rupee coins of higher denominations and establishment of another paper plant in a different geographical region. Jagannathan strongly advocated the increased use of coins, as was the case with some developed countries, to ease the situation. Concluding the letter, Jagannathan stressed that the main recommendations listed above were very important and urgent, not in least the recommendation for a new paper plant; a second plant was inescapable and it took four to five years to plan and get such a plant operating in full production. A copy of the letter was endorsed to M.G. Kaul, economic secretary, Ministry of Finance. The government responded promptly and positively by taking series of measures, but the situation did not improve much till 1981.[4]

The period between 1967 and 1981 was politically very intense. The old ways were giving way to new ones and there was a shift in power too. There were dramatic changes in the institutional setting that resulted in curtailing Central Bank's freedom to influence the key variable of monetary policy, namely, the interest rate. It was a period of direct lending and credit rationing. The tectonic shift that took place was the nationalization of banks, which saw the public-sector banks having an incredibly high share in both bank deposits and bank credit, ranging from 85

---

[3]Ibid. 437.

[4]Ibid. 436–8.

to 90 per cent. A number of other financial institutions also came under the jurisdiction of the public sector during this period. All this altered the nature of the relationship between the government and the RBI, which was left with little say in the structure of the financial system.

One most fundamental characteristic of the period was the RBI's loss of control over the sources of change in money stock. There were no institutional limits on the government for issuing securities and availing of credit from the RBI. It was merely required to accommodate the public borrowing programme with suitable policy adjustments. In other words, whatever the government demanded, the RBI was obliged to give. It was not to reason why.

Jagannathan had managed to keep things stable from 1970. But things started changing very fast. In early 1975, political power in Delhi centred on Indira Gandhi's son, Sanjay, who had started an automobile manufacturing company called Maruti, wanted the credit limit for his company to be increased. However, the RBI had rejected the enhancement since Maruti Motors was not compliant with existing rules for credit enhancement. There were acrimonious exchanges between Jagannathan and the finance ministry on the issue. Jagannathan was due to retire in June 1975. Unable to cope with the situation that was developing, he decided to leave a few weeks before the end of his term. In some quarters, it was alleged that Jagannathan had left because he was in a hurry to get to his next job as India's executive director at the IMF.[5]

The question of the autonomy or independence of the RBI was raised in Parliament during the debate on the RBI (Amendment) Act, 1974. Madhu Limaye, Member of Parliament (MP), stated in his intervention:

---

[5]Srinivasa Raghavan, T.C.A., *A Crown of Thorns: The Governors of the RBI*, Chennai, Westland, 2016, p. 20.

> The second point of deep concern is that this Government has completely usurped the autonomy of the Reserve Bank. I would like to invite your attention to a strange incident that had happened at the Joint Parliamentary Committee of the Financial Institutions. Reserve Bank Governor Shri S. Jagannathan, who is an ICS, had come to give evidence before the Committee. I put a straight question to him as to whether he had submitted his views about this Act to the Government and if so, whether he had any objection to the basic principles of this Act. Reserve Bank Governor who had come to give evidence stated that he would reply to my question after consulting the Government and obtaining their permission. Thus, not only did he insult the Joint Parliamentary Committee but it also reflects the psychology of the Reserve Bank's Governor.[6]

Jagannathan himself was likely uncomfortable at the decimation of the RBI and usurping of its domain by the finance ministry. Perhaps as a final act of defiance, he announced the slack season credit policy of 1975 without consulting the Ministry of Finance, just before he relinquished the office of the governor and handed over charge to N.C. Sen Gupta. It was Sen Gupta who had to face the ire of the finance ministry for this defiance by the RBI.

ANECDOTE: 'BRIDGE' FINANCE[7]

There have been some funny moments in the history of the RBI. It had issued a circular dated 27 March 1973 relating to 'bridge' finance to power sector. It turned out that some state governments

---

[6] *The Reserve Bank of India: Volume 3, 1967–1981*, Mumbai, Central Office, Reserve Bank of India, 2005, pp. 457–8.

[7] Adapted from *The Reserve Bank of India: Volume 3, 1967–1981*, Mumbai, Central Office, Reserve Bank of India, 2005, p. 123.

had interpreted the Bank's permission to extend 'bridge finance' as finance for construction of bridges.[8] This was revealed when the Uttar Pradesh State Bridge Corporation, through the Bank of India and Punjab National Bank (PNB), sought sanction for term loans of ₹40 lakh and ₹22.09 lakh for construction of bridges over Kali Nadi in Farrukhabad and Banaili in Bijnor district, respectively. The Bank had taken the view that bridge construction, being an infrastructure activity, should be financed by the state government through budgetary allocations and that the bank credit for this purpose, if at all given, could only be marginal, say, not exceeding 25 to 30 per cent of the cost of the project. Accordingly, in 1976, approvals were granted for term loans of ₹12 lakh and ₹6.60 lakh to the Bank of India and PNB, respectively. Subsequent demands from the corporation were dealt with similarly.

[8]Bridge finance is a short-term funding arrangement to keep the operations going till the time long term funding arrangements are made.

11

N.C. Sen Gupta

Nirmal Chandra Sen Gupta took charge as interim governor of the RBI on 19 May 1975. He was the eleventh governor of the RBI and held office until 19 August 1975, when K.R. Puri took office as governor. Prior to his appointment as governor, Sen Gupta worked as secretary to the Department of Banking in the Ministry of Finance. His tenure lasted for 92 days, but despite the brevity of his time as governor, his signature appears on the 1,000-rupee note. This is the only note that bears his signature.

Sen Gupta had been appointed governor because the prime minister and finance minister could not agree on who should succeed Jagannathan as governor. The three months he spent in office were largely uneventful and marked by the absence of any policy initiatives. As a final act of defiance, S. Jagannathan had announced the slack-season credit policy of 1975 without consulting the Ministry of Finance just before he handed over charge to Sen Gupta. It is likely that Jagannathan sought to avoid the unfortunate experience of being sidelined by the finance minister as he had been in the previous year, when C. Subramaniam informed public-sector banks of the details of the busy-season credit policy mere days before the RBI's scheduled announcement of the same. It is amusing to think of Sen Gupta leaving the finance ministry, when it was almost his prerogative to be displeased with the RBI, to join the RBI and immediately face the government's displeasure.

Sen Gupta's tenure was also significant for the separation of the UTI from the RBI, with the former being a subsidiary of the latter. The UTI was delinked from the RBI and was placed under the IDBI during Emergency. The idea behind the formation of the UTI had been that the trust should be free of government control, but as the IDBI was directly controlled by the fiannce ministry, this transfer meant that the government could influence the UTI through the IDBI if it so desired. It is unfortunate there is no internal record at the RBI to show whether it had been consulted before the Public Financial Institutions Laws (Amendment) Act was brought before Parliament in 1973, by which the relationship between the RBI and the UTI was terminated. V.G. Pendharkar, former executive director of the RBI and one-time executive trustee of the UTI, had called the delinking of the UTI from the RBI a 'grave mistake', saying that the IDBI's position as a borrower-oriented institution precludes it from being a lender of last resort and taking actions like the RBI, which can guide an investor-oriented institution like the UTI with its comprehensive knowledge of the economy and research capacity.[1]

---

[1]*The Reserve Bank of India: Volume 3, 1967–1981*, Mumbai, Central Office, Reserve Bank of India, 2005, p. 324–5.

12

K.R. Puri

K.R. Puri was the twelfth governor of the RBI, and had hardly any banking experience when he assumed office on 20 August 1975. Unlike his predecessors, Puri was neither a civil servant nor an economist. He was the chairman and managing director of the LIC when he was appointed governor of the RBI. Puri's appointment had been a matter of contention between the finance minister and the prime minister. All the governors before Puri were directly or indirectly associated with the RBI or were on the Bank's Central Board. They were not new to the RBI. The finance minister was against appointing Puri but had to cede to the prime minister's wishes.[1]

Puri's time as governor was a continuous two-year blow to the RBI's integrity. He had been appointed governor at the behest of the prime minister despite strenuous objections on the part of the finance minister, and Puri's actions as governor showed where his loyalties lay. When Puri took over as governor, the standing credit authorization rule was that credit proposals of ₹1 crore and above were sent to the RBI for approval. It was only after this that they could be sanctioned by the board of the bank in question. Puri was swift to raise the limit for credit authorization

[1] *The Reserve Bank of India: Volume 3, 1967–1981*, Mumbai, Central Office, Reserve Bank of India, 2005, p. 111.

of working capital for private-sector borrowers to ₹2 crore. There are no records at the RBI to show why this shockingly brazen decision was taken and why none of Puri's colleagues at the RBI were consulted, but it was to the immediate benefit of Maruti Motors, then led by Sanjay Gandhi.

Soon after the Maruti Motors episode, the RBI began to forgo a security-based approach towards bank credit and move towards a need-based approach instead. Monetary policy had given way to credit rationing, with the aim of making sure that credit reached those who needed it the most. Naturally, it was the government that decided who was the most in need. Officials at the RBI found this difficult to digest. Policy had given way to ad hocism, with constant disagreements between the finance ministry and the RBI over credit rationing that ended with the RBI being forced to toe the line. It was the beginning of a pattern that continued for the entirety of Puri's tenure.

Disagreements between the ministry and the RBI were all but promised, but the RBI was treated with exceptional carelessness in the Puri days. A good example is Indira Gandhi's ambitious 20-point economic programme, a cornerstone of her government. The RBI should have been at the forefront in implementing parts of the programme, but it was repeatedly sidelined by the government. Eventually, Deputy Governor K.S. Krishnaswamy wrote to Banking Secretary N.C. Sen Gupta, objecting to the fact that the RBI had not even been informed that the government had issued instructions to public-sector banks five separate times just during the first half of 1976. Krishnaswamy stressed the need to involve the RBI at least indirectly to avoid confusion and improve coordination, but his words fell on deaf ears. In October 1976, the *Economic Times* reported that the Department of Revenue had assigned the task of coordinating efforts to implement the schemes of the 20-point economic programme to nine public-sector banks. The RBI received this news not from the finance ministry but from the same newspaper report. The banks were to form a bankers' committee for each state. The purpose of these committees was to consider problems that required inter-bank coordination, allocate schemes to be implemented at the district level and bring uniformity in the terms and conditions of credit under specific schemes. The committee members were leaders of banks, chairmen of regional rural banks (RRBs), government agencies and representatives of state cooperative banks and lead development banks. The RBI was neither included nor informed, as a DBOD office note recorded.

Krishnaswamy reiterated the RBI's request that the government issue instructions to public-sector banks only through the RBI in order to not misrepresent the RBI's role to the banks and the public. He also expressed the RBI's disappointment at being completely sidelined in the execution of the 20-point programme. The government's response was disappointing; it sent the RBI a copy of the circular issued to the public-sector banks and made no attempt to reassure the RBI that its position would be respected in the future. Krishnaswamy, in a note to Puri, wrote that this was 'yet another instance of bypassing of the RBI by the Department'.[2] Puri initialled the note and made no comments.

Puri was clearly not inclined to take issues with the finance ministry, no matter how contentious the situation became. Senior officers at the RBI were treated poorly by the government, and bitterness flowered at the RBI. The government continued to tread on the RBI's toes by writing directly to the nationalized banks and enhancing their lending target to the priority sector to 33.3 per cent of their total advances by the end of the fifth Five-Year Plan.[3] The RBI was kept out of the loop, as was rapidly becoming the norm, no matter how significant the decision. Even when it came

[2]Ibid. 178.

[3]Ibid. 175–9.

to allowing branches to be opened abroad, the RBI was sidelined by the government. On 22 August 1975, two days after Puri took over as the governor of RBI, the Department of Banking conveyed to him the decision taken by the finance minister about the revised procedure in order to expedite decisions. The procedure was that individual proposals to open branches or offices abroad by the public-sector banks should be sent directly to the government, with a copy to the RBI, and these were to be considered by a committee consisting of officials of different ministries and the Bank. This, in effect, meant that the Department of Banking, through this committee, took over the powers vested in the RBI under Section 23 of the Banking Regulation Act.

The RBI could not ward off government criticism that it was unable to restrain money supply. It was in a classic dilemma. The RBI needed to limit money supply expansion, but, at the same time, it needed to provide for priority-sector advances. It was never clear how these ratios were to be defined and there were divergent opinions between the RBI and the finance ministry. In the final analysis, the Bank could not oppose the government, for two possible reasons. One was Emergency and the sudden sidelining of R.K. Hazari, then a deputy governor. The other was that even though the government knew what the RBI had done to tighten money supply, it expected the RBI would take the blame. Eventually, the RBI allowed itself to be passively led by the government and hoped for the best possible outcome.

During Puri's tenure, a very important policy initiative was taken on the foreign-exchange management front. The international exchange rate scenario back then was vulnerable, which ultimately forced the finance ministry to take a historic decision in 1975. The rupee had been pegged to the pound sterling since 1931, except for a brief interlude of three months in September 1971. In order to overcome the weaknesses associated with a single currency peg and to ensure stability of the exchange rate, the rupee was pegged to a basket of currencies with effect from September 1975. The rupee was delinked from the sterling and a new arrangement was adopted under which the exchange value of the rupee was determined with reference to the daily movements of a selected number of currencies of countries, which were major trading partners. Presumably, the basket included the US dollar, the pound sterling, the German mark, the French franc and the Japanese yen. Once again, the major initiative came from the government and the Bank had to toe the government line.

The Janata Party government came to power in the elections that followed Emergency, with H.M. Patel as finance minister. As a result of Puri's close association with the Congress government, he was unceremoniously asked to resign from the RBI. According to M. Narasimham, the then finance secretary, one of the first things H.M. Patel did upon taking charge as finance minister was tell him that Puri had to go, on the express orders of the prime minister. Puri was persona non grata with the prime minister and finance minister, and Narasimham persuaded him to resign.[4]

The Janata Party government did not last long, but among the significant decisions it made while in power was to auction gold in 1978. The idea was to bring down prices of gold and contain gold smuggling. The government would sell gold from both its own holdings of confiscated gold and, through the RBI, gold generated from the government-owned mines at Kolar. The auctions were conducted by the RBI; 12.95 tonnes of gold was sold, bringing in ₹86.69 crore for the government. This was not as satisfactory a result as the government had hoped for, and so it ordered a review of the scheme through a committee headed by Patel. Whatever investigation was intended would be altered by the Congress government's return to power in January 1980

---

[4]Ramachandran, P.P., *RBI: An Anecdotal History*, New Delhi, Academic Foundation, 2016, p. 5.

after the midterm elections. Immediately upon its return, the new government paused the gold jewellery export replenishment scheme. It also ordered an inquiry into whether the confiscated gold (that had now been auctioned off) had been kept separately or mixed with the gold that had been donated by the public as part of the gold bond scheme and whether the Janata Party had allowed its members to participate in the gold auctions. The matter was serious and merited the formation of a one-man committee, and the man chosen to constitute and chair this committee was none other than Puri.

It would be natural to think that being asked to resign from the post of governor would derail Puri's career, but it would be patently false to say so. Since his resignation from the RBI, Puri had become the chairman of the Public Enterprises Selection Board and had received in this appointment an opportunity to settle the score. His appointment was controversial; his removal from the post of governor was relatively recent, and the scope of power he was given under this committee was extraordinary. Subramanian Swamy, MP, had objected to Puri's appointment and enquired about the propriety of Puri probing the actions of a government that had removed him from office. Finance Minister R. Venkataraman had been quick to point out that Puri had not been removed but had sought retirement.

Puri appeared to harbour resentment towards the Janata Party government for his premature removal as governor of the RBI. The Puri Committee submitted its report in 1981, wherein it concluded that the gold auctions during the Janata Party regime were conceived neither in the public interest nor on sound economic considerations. The committee indicted the previous government for 'undue haste' and the RBI for 'undue anxiety' to carry out 'the government's wishes' without any legal authority. It also did not rule out ill intent concerning the scheme. Puri had also forwarded a secret note to the government on 20 April 1981, seeking further investigations. Interestingly, the government then constituted a committee of four senior Cabinet ministers to look into the report. One of the demands it rejected was for the prosecution of H.M. Patel and I.G. Patel for the illegal sale of gold. Another demand, also rejected, was to make public the Puri Committee Report. On 18 September 1981, Venkataraman informed the Parliament that the gold auction might have been 'just an error of judgment'.[5]

In spite of all the ugliness, there were positive developments even in Puri's time as governor. In his memoir, Narasimham writes about putting forth the idea of an agricultural development bank for the agricultural sector. It would be the apex institution for agricultural credit; it would provide project finance, working capital finance and long-term finance to state, central and urban cooperative banks by way of refinancing and it would be an agrarian counterpart to the Industrial Development Bank. Narasimham wrote to Puri seeking his views on the idea in 1976, and it was implemented in 1981 as the National Bank for Agriculture and Rural Development (NABARD).[6] The Asian Clearing Union commenced operations in Puri's tenure, and a new money supply series was introduced. The RRBs were set up when Puri was governor.

[5] *The Reserve Bank of India: Volume 3, 1967–1981*, Mumbai, Central Office, Reserve Bank of India, 2005, p. 423.

[6] Narasimham, M., *From Reserve Bank to Finance Ministry and Beyond: Some Reminiscences*, New Delhi, UBS Publishers' Distributors, 2002, p. 88.

13

M. Narasimham

Maidavolu Narasimham was the thirteenth governor of the RBI from 2 May 1977 to 30 November 1977. His appointment was meant to be a stopgap measure until I.G. Patel finished his term with the United Nations Development Programme (UNDP) and take up the office of governor, but the seven months he spent leading the RBI ended up being profoundly productive and memorable for both the RBI and India.

Narasimham was the grandson of Dr Sarvepalli Radhakrishnan, former president of India. Born in Bangalore, he studied economics at Presidency College in Chennai and St. John's College, Cambridge, UK. Narasimham was the first governor to be appointed from the ranks of the RBI itself, having joined the RBI as a research officer in the economics department. He later joined the government and served as secretary to the Ministry of Finance. A reformist, Narasimham chaired the Committee on the Financial System, established in 1991 when the Indian government decided to open up the economy. In 1998, Narasimham led the Committee on Banking Sector Reforms, and he is fondly remembered as the father of banking reforms in India.

Narasimham's intelligence and acumen first caught the attention of Governor H.V.R. Iengar while the former worked in the RBI as a research officer. After interacting more closely with the Government of India, he was soon drafted to work in the government. Narasimham's interest in real banking and credit dovetailed neatly with the government's desire to step up rural and agricultural credit. It had been a matter of concern for years: Commercial banks did not stand to gain anything from opening branches in rural areas and so did not make a move towards it. Narasimham, then additional secretary to the Department of Economic Affairs, suggested setting up RRBs after a discussion with C. Subramaniam, then finance minister. In July 1975, the Indira Gandhi government constituted a working group to examine the feasibility of setting up new rural banks as subsidiaries of public-sector banks, hoping to cater to the needs of people in rural India. The group was chaired by Narasimham and submitted its report on 31 July 1975, leading to the 1975 ordinance that allowed RRBs to be established in India.

Two developments in Narasimham's tenure had considerable implications for monetary and credit policy. The first, which occurred in June 1977, was in connection with the financial assistance for monopoly procurement of cotton in Maharashtra. The Maharashtra State Co-operative Marketing Federation wanted a monopoly over the purchase of cotton. It also wanted to trade in that commodity not for the stabilization of raw cotton prices or for equitable distribution of incomes among cotton growers but primarily for profit. The RBI could not endorse this monopolistic operation as it went against its policy of support for state cooperative banks. Having made it clear to the government of Maharashtra that it would not provide any direct refinancing assistance to this scheme, the RBI also did not permit the Maharashtra State Cooperative Bank (MSCB) to lend funds to this scheme. Matters escalated and soon involved Prime Minister Morarji Desai. Narasimham explained the RBI's stance to Desai, and also made it clear that the resources of the MSCB were already stretched thin and needed to be directed to assist productive credit through the cooperative system. Desai agreed with the RBI's point of view and, consequently, the possible emergence of such schemes in different states was also nipped in the bud. At least for the moment, the RBI ensured that credit policy remained on track.[1]

The second development concerned the bifurcation of savings deposits into demand liability and time liability portions. Under Regulation 7 of the Reserve Bank of India's Scheduled Banks' Regulations 1951, the maximum amount that could be withdrawn from savings bank accounts without prior notice was regarded as a demand liability, and any excess over this amount as a time liability. Since banks were free to decide on the maximum amounts of withdrawal from savings accounts, several banks reported all or a larger part of their savings deposits as demand liabilities. This resulted in distorted data and, in October 1977, the RBI declared this method unrealistic. Instead, the average monthly minimum balances arrived at for crediting interest should be treated as time liabilities and the rest of the amount as demand liabilities. The RBI's suggestion was consistent with the recommendation of the working group on money supply. Narasimham, therefore, paved the way for a more meaningful concept of money supply.

While he was the governor of the RBI, Narasimham foresaw serious troubles for India in the prices of oil, then spiralling due to the Gulf War. Considering it a prudent time to approach the IMF for a medium-term loan, Narasimham did so and was ensured a positive response if India approached the IMF for such a loan informally. He requested Finance Minister R. Venkataraman to consider drawing from the IMF's extended fund facility, but neither Venkataraman nor the economic affairs secretary was interested. Narasimham then brought up the subject with the prime minister and explained India's deteriorating external

---

[1] *The Reserve Bank of India: Volume 3, 1967–1981*, Mumbai, Central Office, Reserve Bank of India, 2005, p. 400.

payments position. If India wanted to maintain measures taken to liberalize imports and deregulate industry, then it was only wise to seek the IMF's assistance at the earliest, while India was still in a position of strength and could argue for better conditions on the loan. The prime minister understood and accepted his argument, and instructed him to work out a proposal and leave a note with her secretary. A few months later, the government decided to formally nominate Narasimham to the post of executive director at the IMF.[2] Narasimham's prescience is reflected in the fact that India did approach the IMF at the right time and successfully avoided a balance of payments crisis. India's stance in favour of a reasonable blend of multilateral borrowing and financial credit proved to be right in the light of later events. Furthermore, the fact that India approached the IMF before it got into a deep crisis was a feather in the cap for both the RBI and the IMF. Jacques De Larosière de Champfeu, managing director of the IMF at the time, recalled with a sense of pride the IMF's loan of 1981 as an achievement of his tenure.[3]

Narasimham's enthusiasm and creativity made him an innovative leader and an excellent problem solver. Some of his ideas, which have since been discontinued, include the CAS and the National Credit Council. Narasimham also introduced the trade-weighted basket of currencies that determined the exchange rate until 1992, moving away from the exchange rate pegged to the sterling. It was also Narasimham's suggestion to Sir Benegal Rama Rau that led to the establishment of the Refinancing Corporation, which was eventually absorbed into the IDBI.

A delightful anecdote involving the London branch of the Central Bank of India reveals Narasimham's method of solving problems. In 1970, a bill discounting fraud of £18,55,400 was

---

[2]Ibid. 655–6.

[3]Ibid. 657–8.

detected at the London branch of the Central Bank of India during an inspection by an RBI team. The fraud was technically committed by Sami J. Patel, the manager of the branch, but it also involved three British banks and a group of companies owned by a former deputy governor of the RBI, Sir Cecil R. Trevor. Narasimham, then secretary to the RBI's Central Board, was dispatched to London to meet the deputy governor of the Bank of England. The deputy governor who was in charge of discount operations maintained a threatening posture right from the beginning, to take 'severe action against (the) errant institutions', but was clearly referring to the Central Bank of India. Narasimham pointed out that the Central Bank of India was 'not sinning, but [was] sinned against'.[4] When the executive from Bank of England continued to make threats, Narasimham pointed out that as the Central Bank of India had recently been nationalized, any punitive action by the Bank of England could have political repercussions. He then switched tactics and told the officer that the RBI had reason to believe that a couple of British banks were also transgressing exchange control regulations in India. But the RBI had been considerate of the cordial relationship between British and Indian banks and between the Bank of England and the RBI. Having not taken action against these British banks, the RBI now expected the Bank of England to return the favour. In the hands of a lesser negotiator, this could have gone terribly awry, but it worked. The officer understood the veiled threat, and the Bank of England did not take action against the Central Bank of India.[5]

Like many governors of the RBI, Narasimham was conscious of the fact that the RBI's relationship with the government was foundational to its functioning. He wrote a report on the RBI and its independence as an institution, noting that the

---

[4]Ibid. 259.
[5]Ibid. 256–61.

Douglas Committee in the USA had recommended that the US Federal Reserve should have autonomy within the government. This concept of central banks being autonomous within the government structure continues to be part of current conventional wisdom. There cannot be two centres of economic power in a society. Even within Narasimham's relatively brief but eventful tenure, there had been moments of conflict and cooperation with the government. It was a matter that merited such contemplation.

Narasimham famously said that whenever India meets a problem, it sets up a committee and starts an institution. He was central to the formation of many committees and chaired many of them to boot. Among these, the Narasimham Committee-I and Narasimham Committee-II on financial reforms are his crowning contributions. The two committees were appointed by the Government of India to review the working of the commercial banks and other financial institutions in the country as well as to suggest measures to remodel these institutions for raising their efficiency.

The first Narasimham Committee Report (1991) made many recommendations concerning the potential reform of the banking sector. The core premise of these recommendations was that the resources of banks should be deployed in the most rational manner, which is the one that provides the greatest benefit to its depositors. These recommendations included a deregulation of interest rates; a phased reduction in the SLR and the phased achievement of an 8 per cent capital adequacy ratio; lifting the bar on setting up new banks in the private sector and abolishing the licensing procedure for branch expansion. The government lost no time in implementing these and other recommendations made by the committee. It also appointed another committee to be chaired by Narasimham in 1998, better known as the Banking Sector Committee.

The second Narasimham Committee focussed on various

areas such as capital adequacy, bank mergers and bank legislation. It submitted its report in April 1998 with further groundbreaking recommendations that included merging Indian banks, thereby enabling them to better handle problems regarding domestic liquidity and exchange rate management; raising capital adequacy norms; further autonomy for banks in their working and an urgent review and possible amendment of laws governing banking in India, like the RBI Act, the SBI Act, and others. Many of these recommendations have already been implemented. Certain recommendations, such as the one urging the merging of Indian banks, have sparked several rounds of discussion. We are currently witnessing a merger drive, with numerous banks having been merged recently to create global-sized banks. Other recommendations, such as those urging technological modernization, professionalism in banking and the depoliticization of banks remain relevant concerns today.

The government was immensely receptive to the Narasimham Committee reports and the recommendations therein, but there was also criticism from certain quarters. Trade unions and bank employees, as well sections of politicians and officials, were critical of the recommendations but did not quite consider that the spirit of competition and other structural changes were necessary to survive. Working under a protective system for a prolonged period can destroy the spirit of productivity and growth, and the success of the committee's recommendations reveals their necessity.

Narasimham appears to have been universally well regarded. Robert McNamara, chief of the World Bank, wrote to Narasimham upon the news of the latter's transfer from the World Bank Board to the IMF Board:

> Your dedication, your consistently thoughtful and informed views, your careful judgement, your breadth of vision and your dogged hard work have all combined to set a standard

> of service on the Board that deserves the gratitude, not only of India and your other constituencies but of the entire development community itself.[6]

Narasimham's colleague and former SBI chairman D.N. Ghosh describes him as enigmatic and creative, bogged down by the weight of tradition as governor. He writes warmly of Narasimham's wit and imagination. Narasimham made friends wherever he went; he served as vice-president-Cooperation of the Asian Development Bank (ADB) for three years. The president of the bank, Masao Fujioka, was keen that Narasimham continue with the ADB and refused to consider another name for his post. His visionary policies and helpful attitude ensured that he is still fondly remembered by his associates at the ADB. Narasimham was honoured with many degrees and awards, including the Padma Vibhushan in 2000. He died in Hyderabad on 20 April 2021 at the age of 94.

TRIVIA

1. Urjit Patel was the eighth deputy governor of the RBI to be made governor, the last being Y.V. Reddy. The RBI's second governor, Sir James Taylor, was the first to be elevated to the position of governor. His successor Sir C.D. Deshmukh was also deputy governor before he became governor following the premature death of his predecessor. K.G. Ambegaokar, another deputy governor, was appointed as the interim governor for about one-and-a-half months in 1957 until H.V.R. Iengar could take over the reins of the RBI. B.N. Adarkar, also a deputy governor, held the post of governor until S. Jagannathan could take over. Amitav Ghosh was the deputy governor from 1982; he was appointed as the governor for a brief period of 20 days

[6]Ibid. 656.

in 1985 until R.N. Malhotra could take over. On the other hand, C. Rangarajan, before his appointment as the governor in December 1992, held charge as deputy governor for over a decade. Reddy also had a six-year tenure as deputy governor before becoming RBI governor in 2003.

2. In 1935, the Secretary of State for India proposed that Sir James Taylor should resign from the ICS when taking up the deputy governorship of the RBI, apparently to ensure the independence of the governor and the deputy governor. In 1953, the government had wanted to review this condition and exempt civil servants from being appointed as deputy governors from its application. However, the Central Board of the RBI was not in favour of such exemption and the proposal was dropped. The government did not pursue the matter further. Therefore, most civil servants have been appointed as governors or deputy governors only after their retirement from ICS/IAS.

14

I.G. Patel

Dr Indraprasad Gordhanbhai Patel, popularly known as I.G. Patel, was the fourteenth governor of the RBI and served from 1 December 1977 to 15 September 1982. An eminent economist and administrator, he was secretary to the Ministry of Finance and the deputy administrator of the UNDP before joining the RBI. After retiring from the RBI, he became the director of IIMA between 1982 and 1984, after which he assumed the directorship of the London School of Economics and Political Science (1984–90).

Patel was an influential bureaucrat in the finance ministry. When Indira Gandhi decided to nationalize 14 major commercial banks in the country on 19 July 1969, Patel was one of the few people who were consulted. On 18 July, she informed Patel that she had taken the decision to nationalize banks for political reasons. Patel is reported to have given two suggestions to Gandhi: one, that foreign banks should not be nationalized and two, that there was no need to nationalize all banks and it would be better if only the major banks, which accounted for around 90 per cent of the total banking business, were nationalized.[1]

The nationalization of 14 commercial banks was a political

[1]*The Reserve Bank of India: Volume 3, 1967–1981*, Mumbai, Central Office, Reserve Bank of India, 2005, pp. 35–8.

move, implemented in a hurry to settle scores with political rivals and firmly settle Mrs Gandhi in the saddle. Since it was a totally unplanned and hasty move, the results were likely to be disappointing as revealed by the future course of events. As recounted by Patel in his memoir, the first phase of nationalization and its aftermath make for an interesting but painful reading. He narrates:

> By all accounts, the nationalisation of major banks was a great success initially. Apart from the political dividends for Mrs Gandhi, it greatly increased popular confidence in the banking system and thus increased the mobilisation of private savings through banks. The savings so mobilised were also used now for supporting public borrowing as well as for meeting hitherto neglected genuine credit needs. The rot started with the Emergency and the political opportunism started was compounded by bank staff of all grades. With nationalisation came the entry of national unions with allegiance to different political parties, mostly the Congress and the Left. Shielded by political support the bank staff proceeded to create for themselves a vast superstructure of perks and privileges under which they could define and limit work, enforce overstaffing and generally encourage indiscipline and incompetence without any fear of being held accountable. Merit went by the board as did customer service; and seniority and closeness to political power held sway.[2]

In 1980, after Gandhi was voted back to power, there was a second round of nationalization of commercial banks. Six banks—Andhra Bank, Oriental Bank of Commerce (OBC), Corporation Bank, New Bank of India, Punjab & Sind Bank and Vijaya Bank—were

[2]Ibid. 50.

nationalized. Compared to the first nationalization in 1969, it was a low-key affair. In 1969, the RBI was not consulted and Governor L.K. Jha was deeply unhappy with the decision. However, in 1980, the initiative came from Patel, who was the governor of the RBI then. There are no records in the Bank suggestive of any formal correspondence between the Bank and the government on this subject. No discussion appears to have taken place at the meetings of the Central Board of the Bank. However, one gets an insight into what happened from I.G. Patel's memoir. 'Such is the irony of life', he writes, 'that one of the first steps I had to recommend to Mrs Gandhi was that she should nationalise another swathe of private banks'.[3]

He recounted that the RBI had the responsibility to supervise private banks and see that they comply with social control norms as well as with law. Several small private banks had now grown to respectable size and some of them had become the personal fiefdoms of individuals who disregarded all rules and advice with impunity. They were indulging in shady dealings and offering unfair competition to the nationalized banks. As the RBI governor, Patel felt that the only practical way to tackle the problem was to nationalize the banks, which had now reached the cut-off point of the 1969 Act. His advice was readily accepted by Gandhi in spite of her promise to not usher in a new wave of nationalization. Patel added that the prime minister had 'no appetite' for nationalization then and that this particular initiative for the second phase of bank nationalization had come entirely from him as the governor of the RBI.[4]

On becoming the governor on 1 December, Patel took up the issue of branch expansion with a measure of urgency. His preferences were for opening offices in deficit districts, for

---

[3]Ibid.

[4]Ibid. 51.

completely forgoing expansion of offices in metropolitan centres and for cancelling licences that were not utilized. His proposal and plan of action were largely approved by the government.

The procedure for allowing foreign banks to set up branch offices in India or allowing Indian banks to set up branch offices overseas and whether the Ministry of Finance or the RBI should do it were vexatious issues that were creating bitterness for quite some time. In 1975, the government had set up an inter-departmental committee for approval of applications by Indian banks to open branch offices abroad. By doing this, the Department of Banking took over the powers vested in the RBI under Section 23 of the Banking Regulation Act. This was termed as 'encroachment of its territory' in the RBI and there was serious discontent in RBI about such marginalization, particularly, in the eyes of banks.

In February 1978, the questions of granting various applications received from foreign banks the permission to open new branches in India and some new banks wanting entry in India came up again. It was suggested that the applications would be placed for consideration before the existing committee (which considered proposals by Indian banks wanting to open branches abroad). Patel took it as an affront to the RBI's authority. Not wishing to let the government erode the RBI's authority further, he sent a note prepared by Deputy Governor K.S. Krishnaswamy to the government, which stated that 'this is a matter on which the present position is quite unsatisfactory. Every time we put up a memorandum to our Board regarding opening of foreign branches by Indian banks or of Indian branches of foreign banks, we are merely asking the central Board to endorse a government decision. This is not right for either the RBI or the government.'[5] He reiterated that the RBI was the authority to grant the licences under the statute, and the process should, in both form and

[5]Ibid. 217.

substance, conform to the statutory provisions. He expressed the desire to set things right but, at the same time, advised that it should not imply any reduction in the RBI having to consult with, and generally respect the views of, the government. Even with respect to Indian banks wanting to open branches abroad, Patel suggested that only larger banks with expertise in opening branches abroad should be allowed. He also suggested that instead of reviewing each application, there should be a perspective plan for next few years that should be drawn up for Indian banks wishing to open branches abroad. On this, the government asked the RBI to prepare a set of guidelines regarding the future approach towards permitting opening of branches abroad by Indian banks and thereafter prepare a perspective plan for branch expansion. Thus, due to Patel, RBI regained some lost glory. Patel's intention was to ensure that the RBI and the Ministry of Finance did not act at cross-purposes and, more importantly, did not encourage the banks to play the two against each other.[6]

This was also the period when the review of the CAS was undertaken and modifications were made to the working of the scheme with reference to the Chore Committee and Tandon Committee reports on working of cash credit system. In 1978, the Credit Guarantee Corporation of India was taken over by the Deposit Insurance Corporation, and the combined entity was named Deposit Insurance and Credit Guarantee Corporation. Further, credit guarantee scheme relating to the cooperative sector, namely, the Small Loans (Cooperative Credit Societies) Guarantee Scheme, 1982, which provided guarantee cover to select primary agricultural credit societies, primary land development banks and branches of state land development banks with respect to their lending for agricultural and allied activities, was formulated.

---

[6]Ibid. 215–21.

Since 1971, the National Commission on Agriculture was lobbying for setting up an agriculture development bank. In 1976, the government recommended the creation of an all-India institutional framework that could take an integrated view of agricultural and rural credit needs in the country. However, the proposed institute had remained on paper in spite of the pressing need for such an organization. It was Patel, who, along with the deputy governor of the RBI in charge of rural credit, M. Ramakrishnayya, worked out the details of the scheme and, thus, NABARD, came into existence on 12 July 1982 as an apex bank to serve the financing and technical needs of agricultural and rural development activities.

In a reversal of the stand taken by his predecessor, M. Narasimham, that the RBI would not agree to finance monopoly procurement operations, Patel agreed to authorize the MSCB to give a hypothecation cash credit limit of ₹15 crore to the Maharashtra State Cooperative Marketing Federation (MSCMF) for financing the latter's cotton monopoly procurement operations. It was not clear as to why this decision was taken, although it contradicted the restrictive credit policy followed by the RBI back then.

The demonetization of Indian rupee notes of 1,000, 5,000 and 10,000 was undertaken and the gold auctions were held during Patel's tenure. Demonetization of high denomination notes is quite a radical measure and is normally resorted to by governments to counter forgery and illegal printing of notes by unauthorized sources. The Wanchoo Committee on Black Money had recommended demonetization long back but this suggestion was not acted upon since it was suspected that most black money operators had got rid of high value currency notes as huge publicity had been given to the recommendations of the committee. The government resorted to demonetization of 1,000, 5,000- and 10,000-rupee notes on 16 January 1978 under the

High Denomination Bank Notes (Demonetization) Ordinance, 1978. Patel was not very keen on this measure for two reasons: one, it was a political decision targeted at so-called 'corrupt' members of the predecessor political party that had recently lost the general elections and two, he felt that such a measure hardly ever had any significant results. People with black money do not keep their ill-gotten gains or wealth for long in currency notes and convert the same into other asset classes. Therefore, he felt that demonetization was not worth the results that were expected. However, the government did not heed his advice. The result was that over 90 per cent currency was back into the banks and this measure for black money containment was a miserable failure.[7]

The Janata Party government during Patel's tenure as governor sought to implement the sale of gold officially to discourage smuggling. He was not keen and, by his own admission, sought to dissuade the government, although no correspondence is available in this regard. He suggested to the government that the RBI would undertake the operation of selling gold only as an agent of the government, and that it would use confiscated gold, newly mined gold and 'non-returnable gold' acquired through the gold bond scheme and refrain from using official gold reserves. The Budget of 28 February 1978 gave executive authority to the Bank to hold gold auctions.

In retrospect, it can be said that the gold auctions were, at best, a damage-control exercise. The auctions were fairly and objectively conducted. Some sensitive decisions were taken to make them leak proof and to avoid corruption and favouritism. Deputy Governor M. Ramakrishnayya was in charge of the operation and exercised close surveillance over the auctions. In all, 14 auctions were held from 3 May to 23 October 1978, in which 12.95 tonnes of gold

[7]Ibid. 450–3.

were sold to the public, yielding a revenue of ₹86.96 crore.

Patel was a very bold and straightforward person. We get a taste of this when he said that he belonged to an age where central bank governors, like children, were supposed to be seen, not heard. Although they were allowed to smile in public, they had to emulate the Mona Lisa and maintain an aura of mystery!

When it came to the governor's responsibility to speak up, Patel was of the view that when vital questions arise, the governor could not be inactive. He is a public servant with loyalty to the country and the Constitution. He has to choose his battles and fight them valiantly even while being discreet about it. His ultimate defence is democracy and the tradition of free debate. He understood how important the RBI governor's role was as his decisions affected the entire country and, thus, was sensitive to render accountability for actions and results of those actions.

Patel unfolded an approach towards 'growth with social justice'. He put it by saying that the real test of success does not lie merely in opening new branches in the rural areas or increasing the proportion of credit that goes to agriculture or other priority areas. Efforts have to be directed more specifically towards the poorer strata, even in priority sectors. Moreover, the objective is not just to give credit to the poor but to make them more productive and truly creditworthy. He said he was determined to simplify and rationalize the regulatory mechanism.[8]

Patel passed away in New York on 17 July 2005. He was 80 years old. He was remembered reverently by prominent politicians Meghnad Desai and Robert McNamara. He was awarded the Padma Vibhushan in 1991. The post of I.G. Patel Professor of Economics and Government was created in his honour at the London School of Economics.

---

[8]Ibid. 401.

15

Manmohan Singh

Dr Manmohan Singh was the fifteenth governor of the RBI, serving from 16 September 1982 to 14 January 1985. He is the only governor of the RBI who rose to become first the finance minister of the country and then the prime minister of India.

Singh was born in Gah, a village now in Pakistan. After the partition of India, his family migrated to Amritsar. Singh studied economics at Hindu College and then at Punjab University. Singh earned his master's degree in 1954, and attended St. John's College in University of Cambridge to complete the Economics Tripos programme. He later attended Nuffield College in the University of Oxford, UK, for his doctorate in economics. Singh worked for the United Nations Conference on Trade and Development (UNCTAD) from 1966 to 1969, and then returned to India to teach at the Delhi School of Economics. Soon after leaving the institution to join the government as an economic advisor in the Ministry of Commerce, Singh caught the attention of Lalit Narayan Mishra, who hired him as an advisor in the Ministry of Foreign Trade. He went on to hold key posts in the government, such as the chief economic advisor in the Ministry of Finance, before eventually becoming governor of the RBI from 1982 to 1985.

Singh played a significant role in shaping the RBI and had an eventful tenure as its governor. In his inaugural address, he spoke of the inherent necessity of harmoniously integrating monetary and fiscal policies. In order for monetary restraint to achieve its objective, monetary policy could not be overburdened, and the same held true for the fiscal system. The latter had to be operated in a manner such that there was no excessive need to rely on the RBI to finance public expenditure. It was both a challenge and an opportunity for Singh to achieve growth while maintaining price stability and a viable balance of payments.[1]

Much of what Singh articulated as the need of the hour remains the need of the hour today. Singh's prescience was on display in 1984 when he spoke of the need to meet the credit needs of hitherto neglected sections of the population and anti-poverty programmes like the Integrated Rural Development Programme. He called for greater efficiency in the banking system and better customer service through new work technology, manpower planning and training arrangements. These would in turn help the banking sector to maintain price stability and manage the balance of payments. All these, and ensuring the profitability of banking operations, were the responsibilities he identified for himself as governor of the RBI.

True to his word, Singh promoted rural development in his time at the RBI. Most significantly, the NABARD commenced operations on 12 July 1982. Singh believed firmly that the RBI could not be passive in ensuring the health of the agrarian sector, particularly when it was from where 40 per cent of the GDP originated. It was the duty of the RBI to assist in alleviating poverty, and the NABARD was the arm through which it would do this.[2]

Singh had a far-reaching impact on the conduct of monetary policy for years to come. It was in his tenure as governor that the Sukhamoy Chakravarty Committee was set up to undertake

---

[1]*The Reserve Bank of India: Volume 4, 1981–1997*, New Delhi, Academic Foundation in Association with Reserve Bank of India, 2013, pp. 44–5.
[2]Ibid. 360.

a critical review of India's monetary system and its interface with fiscal policy, especially its relationship with debt financing and fiscal debt management. The committee was also asked to examine the market instruments that could be developed to improve credit policy transmission and strengthen policy formulation. The committee's 1985 report, authored by C. Rangarajan, became the blueprint for India's monetary and economic policies for the future. Its main recommendation was that both the government and the RBI should show due concern for the achievement of price stability; government actions must be aimed at raising output levels and the RBI's actions should relate to the control of expansion in the money reserve and money supply. In layman's terms, this meant that the RBI should keep a strict watch on the government's borrowings, especially deficit financing.

It is difficult for a principled man to survive in government, and, thus, Singh often ran into problems with the government on this front, sometimes to a degree so severe that the RBI almost lost its power to license banks. Two episodes stand out as examples of Singh standing up to the government to assert the RBI's integrity and autonomy, only to make peace later: the Bank for Credit and Commerce International (BCCI) episode and the Swraj Paul episode.

The first event is centred on the BCCI. Founded in 1972 with head offices in Karachi and London, the BCCI had expanded by 1980 and had 150 branches in over 40 countries. In 1977, it applied to the RBI for permission to open two branches in India. Then governor I.G. Patel advised the government against granting the BCCI the permission it sought; he suspected the bank's activities were not above board, and its immediate astronomical success was the result of both poor regulation and unsavoury activities like money laundering, arms dealing and funding terrorism. Still, the bank was allowed to open a representative office to liaise, if not conduct business. Two years later, a junior minister sanctioned the opening of a BCCI branch on the last day of the Morarji Desai government. Singh was the secretary, economic affairs, at the time and was strongly against this decision. He informed Patel, who was quick to convince Prime Minister Charan Singh to revoke the order. Singh was not as lucky when the matter came up again in 1983, when he was the governor of the RBI. The Congress government cleared the BCCI to operate in India despite Singh objecting on the grounds that the BCCI was an undesirable and unstable entity to be introduced into India's financial system. The RBI was forced to grant the BCCI the license it sought upon the government's insistence, and Singh was proven right in his convictions when the bank collapsed within a few years.[3]

The second story concerns the investments of Swraj Paul, a British Indian business magnate and a close friend of Indira Gandhi, then prime minister of India. In 1982, the Indian government had announced a portfolio investment scheme for non-resident Indians (NRIs) to encourage foreign investment under certain conditions. Paul and his family were majority shareholders in the London-based Caparo group of companies and began to secretly buy shares in Escorts Ltd. The RBI had not permitted the Caparo group to do so and intended to reject its application, and it had conveyed the same to the finance ministry. The RBI was justifiably afraid that it would be difficult to enforce foreign-exchange regulations given the ownership of the Caparo group, but the government ordered the RBI to grant it permission anyway. Matters escalated once the Caparo group was legitimately involved. The owners of Escorts sensed a takeover and filed a writ petition in the Bombay High Court to successfully get relief against the government order and the RBI's permission. But when the case reached the Supreme Court, it ruled that the order and

---

[3]Ibid. 240–1.

permission were both legally valid and awarded the government and the RBI their respective costs of litigation.

The Swraj Paul case was splashed all over the media, to the consternation of Supreme Court Justice Chinnappa Reddy. Justice Reddy found it 'deplorable' that Paul did not appear before the court and almost rued Singh's propriety, which held him back from going to the press and involving himself in the controversy as readily as Paul did. The judgment also ruled that the RBI changed its position after consultations with the government, and that this could not reasonably be construed as crumbling under pressure.[4] For his part, Singh did not offer any clarification on the matter for years. He did not defend himself to the public; he said that he had spoken for the RBI and the government was welcome to overrule the RBI's opinion in what was necessarily a government scheme.

Singh valued his integrity and tried his best to protect the autonomy of the RBI. When the Cabinet decided that the power of the RBI to issue licenses to branches of foreign banks should be taken away, Singh sent his letter of resignation to Finance Minister Pranab Mukherjee and Prime Minister Indira Gandhi. Later, he managed to persuade Indira Gandhi that the Cabinet decision was not proper. The idea was not implemented and was eventually forgotten altogether.

Singh took a humane approach to managing the strikes that had plagued the RBI since the tenure of his predecessor, I.G. Patel. Though the union strikes had formally ended, industrial relations at the RBI were still poor. Singh reinstated many of the people who had been sacked for joining the strikes, including Suryakant Mahadik, who led the trade union backed by the Shiv Sena. Industrial relations at the RBI began to improve almost immediately, even though Singh was heavily criticized for the

---

[4]Mukherjee, Pranab, *India—The Turbulent Years: 1980–1996*, New Delhi, Rupa Publications, 2016, pp. 41–7.

decision to reinstate Mahadik. Singh understood that much of his job was human relations, and a rigid bureaucratic approach would be counterproductive. Daman Singh writes:

> A relationship of antagonism cannot be very productive. He tried to understand the workers and reached out to them. He chose to look at the human side of problems—why do people have certain feelings; how can we deal with them as human beings. He said that giving them another chance was not giving into the situation but the hope that there would be a response from the other side. And there was a response.[5]

This was typical of Singh, who believed that strength came from conduct and conviction rather than empty words. Deeply invested in social issues, he spoke to the workers on a number of occasions on matters ranging from alcoholism to tuberculosis. Singh was down to earth; he disliked being treated as an emperor when he visited any state capital as governor as much as he disliked the government's attempts to downplay the importance of the governor and the RBI. For all his inherent contradictions—a bureaucrat who valued humility and the humble man, an academic who would enter politics—Singh was respected by his peers in the government. Despite their disagreements, Pranab Mukherjee wrote that he never saw his rare differences with Singh as any other than 'legitimate exchanges of opinion over professional matters'.[6] Y.V. Reddy also speaks glowingly of Singh as an economist in *Advice and Dissent*, musing that unlike many economists, Singh was always in India and that gave him an advantage.

Singh's tenure at the RBI was relatively short. After two-and-

---

[5]Singh, Daman, *Strictly Personal: Manmohan and Gursharan*, Harper Collins Publishers India, 2014, p. 160.

[6]Mukherjee, Pranab, *India—The Turbulent Years: 1980–1996*, New Delhi, Rupa Publications, 2016, pp. 45.

a-half years of being governor, he went on to become the deputy chairman of the Planning Commission (1985–87). After a series of significant and varied appointments, Singh became the finance minister in 1991 under P.V. Narasimha Rao. Singh had entered politics amidst a severe economic crisis and was credited with freeing India from the burdensome License Raj that had been slowing economic growth and fuelling corruption for decades. The liberalization of the Indian economy, which happened partly due to pressure from the World Bank and the IMF, helped to dramatically hasten development.

Singh was known as much for his academic brilliance as for his quiet dignity and sobriety, traits which would continue to define his political career. His appointment as the finance minister had somehow been a surprise to almost everybody, but Jairam Ramesh writes that no professional economist that worked at the ministry had matched Singh's brilliance and capability, including Shanmukham Chetty, John Mathai and Sir C.D. Deshmukh.[7] Yet Singh had not been Rao's first choice for finance minister; it was I.G. Patel he had wanted, but Patel had declined the offer and suggested Singh instead. Rao had been doubtful as to whether Singh would enter politics, but Singh had taken the plunge and lived up to Rao's expectations.

It also fell on Singh to implement the agenda of the Chandrashekhar government, the minority government before Rao's, which had fallen after the Rajiv Gandhi-led Congress withdrew support. General elections were held soon after, and sympathy extended to the Congress after Rajiv Gandhi's assassination won them the elections. It was somewhat ironic: Singh had served as the deputy chairman of the Planning Commission under Gandhi, who did not consider the body to be of much value. Former Home Secretary C.G. Somiah recalls

---

[7]Ramesh, Jairam, *To the Brink and Back: India's 1991 Story*, New Delhi, Rupa Publications, 2016, p. 35.

the conflict between Gandhi's vision and Singh's pragmatism. Gandhi, as prime minister, was ex-officio chairman of the Planning Commission. When presenting the seventh Five-Year Plan, Gandhi described his vision of autobahns and airfields, speedy trains and shopping malls, entertainment centres and modern hospitals. This was the India for which he wanted the Commission to plan. Singh, at the next meeting, was firm on the negative economic indicators that abounded in India, things that could not be ignored in favour of more dazzling goals. Gandhi did not appreciate this and called the Commission 'a bunch of jokers' when speaking to journalists a few days later, saying they had no understanding of modern development. Singh was terribly hurt, but C.G. Somiah (who was then member secretary of the Planning Commission) persuaded him to stay on.

Singh's surprising foray into politics did not end after his time as finance minister. He has been a member of the Rajya Sabha since 1991, and was the leader of the Opposition until 2004, when he was sworn in as prime minister. He held the office until 2014 and ushered in many projects that aimed at greater social equality and economic stability, such as the Rural Health Mission, Rural Employment Guarantee Scheme and the Right to Information Act. Singh encouraged growth in the Indian market and replaced sales tax with value-added tax. His comprehensive economic reforms have won much recognition over the world, and he is inextricably tied with liberalization in the popular view of those turbulent years.

The facts of Singh's life and work present a picture of a man ill-suited to politics, yet Singh survived in politics much longer than other inexperienced contenders would have. An article by Vivek Kaul attributes this longevity to Singh rarely exceeding his brief and being a team player.[8] This seems a likely explanation;

---

[8]Kaul, Vivek. 'Why Manmohan Didn't Quit Even after Rajiv Called Him a Joker',

flying in the face of Singh's reputed personal integrity, the second United Progressive Alliance (UPA-II) government faced a slew of corruption charges regarding the Commonwealth Games, the 2G spectrum allocation and the allocation of coal blocks.

Singh currently represents Rajasthan in the Rajya Sabha. He has received many honours and awards, including the Padma Vibhushan, India's second highest civilian honour. He is married to Gursharan Kaur and has three daughters with her, including the historian Upinder Singh.

TRIVIA

1. Sir James Taylor is the only governor to have died while in office.
2. The following governors did not sign bank notes: Sir Osborne Smith, K.G. Ambegaokar and Amitav Ghosh.
3. M. Narasimham was the first and so far the only governor to be appointed from the cadres of the RBI, having joined the RBI as a research officer in the Department of Economics in April 1950.
4. The following governors came from the Civil Service: Sir James Taylor, Sir C.D. Deshmukh, Sir Benegal Rama Rau, K.G. Ambegaokar, H.V.R. Iengar, L.K. Jha, S. Jagannathan, I.G. Patel, Manmohan Singh, R.N. Malhotra, S. Venkataramanan, Y.V. Reddy, D. Subbarao and Shaktikanta Das.
5. The following governors have obtained doctorates: Dr I.G. Patel, Dr Manmohan Singh, Dr C. Rangarajan, Dr Bimal Jalan, Dr Y.V. Reddy, Dr D. Subbarao, Dr Raghuram Rajan and Dr Urjit Patel.

Vivek Kaul, 19 July 2012, https://bit.ly/3xNun3f. Accessed on 1 February 2023.

16

Amitav Ghosh

Amitav Ghosh was the governor of the RBI for 20 days in 1985, making his the shortest term of any RBI governor. He was appointed governor as a stop-gap arrangement before R.N. Malhotra joined the RBI as governor. He was the sixteenth governor of the RBI and served from 15 January to 4 February 1985.

With the exception of those 20 days before Malhotra took over as governor, Ghosh's time at the RBI was served entirely as deputy governor. He had an illustrious career in banking before joining the RBI: he was chairman of Allahabad Bank and was also a director of the IDBI. Ghosh also served as a member of the governing body of the National Institute of Bank Management (NIBM). After the appointment of Malhotra, Ghosh returned to his position as deputy governor. He made crucial contributions in the area of banking regulation and supervision. In March 1982, he chaired a committee appointed by the RBI that laid the foundation for strengthening regulatory and supervisory practices in commercial banks in the early stages of their establishment. The recommendations of the Ghosh Committee included a health code system of classification of assets, provisioning and income recognition norms. This paved the way for further reforms in assessing the credit risks of banks' loan portfolios. Ghosh also chaired a working group to assess the logistics of implementing the 1982 20-point economic programme. The group identified the beneficiaries and the type of assistance that could be rendered. It also stressed the need to ensure that the schemes for the beneficiaries were viable and that there was effective coordination between the state governments and banks. He died on 16 September 2020 at age the age of 90.

17

R.N. Malhotra

Ram Narain Malhotra served as the seventeenth governor of the RBI from 4 February 1985 to 22 December 1990. He served as the governor when Rajiv Gandhi was the prime minister and gave a reform orientation to the RBI. His tenure saw the widening of the money market in India and introduction of new instruments recommended by the Sukhamoy Chakravarty Committee on the monetary system and Vaghul's Working Group on the money market. This was the period when the stage for reforms in the money and credit markets was set along with the the consolidation and diversification of banking and non-banking businesses. He persistently pursued the issue of fiscal consolidation with the government. This period also saw invaluable and crucial role played in carrying forward the early reforms by Deputy Governor C. Rangarajan in the areas of monetary and credit policy and research and Amitav Ghosh in the area of banking regulation and supervision.

Rajiv Gandhi brought with him an infectious optimism for change and not even Malhotra was immune. However, he held on to his scepticism, hard won from years of experience as finance secretary that had taught him the secrets of government finances and political imperatives. He remained old school about certain things, and if he had had his way, the budget deficit would have been kept to zero or close enough. It was he who had steered India's finances through the IMF loan years of 1982–84. However, his stewardship of the RBI since 1985 had received mixed responses. In an interview he had said, among other things, that the RBI would endeavour to maintain the autonomy of the institution but that it has to also perform its functions as the monetary authority. He went on to say that the major concerns were systemic. The interest rate was only one area that had been associated with liberalization in the public's mind.[1]

In 1985, the Rajiv Gandhi government unveiled the Long Term Fiscal Policy, a pathbreaking move. It promised fiscal discipline and improvement in direct taxes. This meant lowering of credit to the government by the RBI. The government lowered tax rates, diluted the Monopolistic and Restrictive Trade Practice Act (MRTP) Act and opened many non-strategic industries for investment by the private sector. This reform process was picked up by the RBI too. It decided to give some leeway to commercial banks in fixing deposit rates. In April 1985, the RBI allowed banks to determine the maturity structure of their liabilities and, accordingly, with effect from 8 April 1985, banks were given the discretion to fix interest rates on deposits of maturities of less than one year within a ceiling of 8 per cent. But to Malhotra's dismay, banks could not handle the freedom. Some of them started offering 8 per cent even for 15 days, which started being followed by other banks. This created panic in the finance ministry and, in few days, the measure was withdrawn. Malhotra was furious at this panicky reaction, as he felt that the banks needed to be given more time, but he could do nothing.[2]

---

[1]Taneja, Shiv, 'RBI Has Had Very Good Relations with North Block: R.N. Malhotra', *India Today*, 15 November 1990, https://bit.ly/41eL4C6. Accessed on 31 January 2023.

[2]Srinivasa Raghavan, T.C.A., 'Interest Rate Deregulation: Nugget from History', *Hindu Businessline*, 6 May 2011, https://bit.ly/3YF9ToT. Accessed on 31 January 2023.

At the golden jubilee celebrations of the RBI on 1 June 1985, Malhotra stated that while trying to meet the requirements of a growing economy, the RBI must continue to strive for price stability through its monetary and credit policies. He added that considering the requirements of the seventh Five-Year Plan and the difficult resources position, continued coordination of fiscal and monetary policies and optimal burden-sharing between them would be crucial. The finance minister, V.P. Singh, was more forthcoming in his presidential address on the occasion. He said that fiscal deficits had a direct bearing on money supply and, therefore, a high degree of coordination was necessary between fiscal and monetary policies, so that money supply growth was kept within limits and the overall economic policy framework rested on a proper integration of its important components such as fiscal policy, monetary policy, foreign trade policy and industrial policy. Prime Minister Rajiv Gandhi, speaking at the event on this issue, lauded the RBI for being not only a controlling point for banks but also one of the key inputs for the government on how to run its finances and how to control various financial aspects of the economy.

Unfortunately, what was said by the prime minister was not followed in practice. No governor before Malhotra had had to face the scale of fiscal irresponsibility that the government had then unleashed. The huge budget deficits it began to run up from 1987 caused the crises of 1990 and 1991. Malhotra repeatedly warned about it throughout 1987 to 1990 but was not heard. The problem became even more acute as the current account deficit widened and short-term debt to finance imports shot up. To top it off, there was the issue of repayment to the IMF of the Extended Funded Facility (EFF) loan.

In 1986, S. Venkitaramanan became the new finance secretary who rescued the country as the RBI governor in 1991. The crisis had erupted as a result of his own actions as finance secretary. In

1986, Venkitaramanan promised Gandhi that he had the solution for the deficit problem and came up with two possible sources for augmenting government revenue. One was increasing the SLR, by which the RBI would give the government cheap loans, and the other was the transfer of the RBI's profits to the government, the economic effect of which was nothing but deficit financing. Malhotra, in a long and patronizing note, said no to both. Like Manmohan Singh in 1984, Malhotra objected to a higher SLR saying that it would fuel inflation and would leave less for the banks to lend to industries. However, the government ignored his objections. With regard to transferring RBI profits, he wrote that it was not the same as transfer of normal profits from a public-sector unit; it amounted to increasing RBI credit to the government. Malhotra said that higher transfers would impact the economy adversely and that the government should not consider this 'as an avenue for augmenting resources'. When Venkitaramanan insisted, Malhotra decided to brief the prime minister directly. However, Gandhi called off the meeting at the last minute, which left no choice for Malhotra but to express his reservations to the finance minister, V.P. Singh, and the deputy chairman of the Planning Commission, Manmohan Singh.[3]

Malhotra warned the government and the prime minister that growth in money supply had been too high since early 1987, before the country started feeling the heat of the political problems in the aftermath of the exposure of the Bofors scandal. He reminded the prime minister of the huge increase in bank credit to government, which was not what had been agreed upon between the RBI and the government the previous year. In January 1989, he took the unusual step of directly addressing his concerns to the government and the policy dilemma before the RBI on the vexing issue of

[3]Srinivasa Raghavan, T.C.A., 'RBI-Govt Tussles Are Not New', *Rediff.com*, 20 November 2018, https://bit.ly/3S43AJb. Accessed on 31 January 2023.

the impact of government budget proposals on monetary policy. He articulated his views in a letter written to the then finance minister, S.B. Chavan, on 7 January 1989:

> Monetary policy has to ensure the twin objectives of maintaining reasonable price stability and meeting the genuine credit requirements necessary to support the growth of output. The large and recurring Government budget deficits have been contributing to strong monetary expansion and over time, there has been serious erosion in the effectiveness of monetary policy instruments. In the context of the large budget deficits, it is difficult to control monetary expansion which, in turn, contributes to inflation.[4]

In another letter dated 18 December 1989, he wrote to the finance minister:

> [W]hat started off as a mechanism for providing temporary accommodation to the Central Government to enable it to maintain a minimum balance with the Reserve Bank became an open-ended monetisation of budgetary deficits, thus substantially undermining the role and effectiveness of monetary policy. What is more, the Treasury Bill which is a short-term instrument for meeting temporary needs has been used for financing the long-term requirements of the Government.[5]

The only solution, in his view, was to rein in the budget deficit by impounding more cash from the banks via a higher CRR. He felt that the economy could not afford excess liquidity sloshing around and pushing the price level up. The RBI outlined a few radical proposals to remedy the situation, such as promoting

[4] *The Reserve Bank of India: Volume 4, 1981–1997*, New Delhi, Academic Foundation in Association with Reserve Bank of India, 2013, p. 50.

[5] Ibid. 67.

an explicit amendment to the RBI Act, whereby the RBI was not to be subject to any direction by the government regarding RBI's holdings of government securities; a progressive reduction in the overall budget deficit spread over the next three years; longer-term resource requirements of the government to be met through floatation of dated securities and not treasury bills; a limit to be fixed on the outstanding level of ways and means advances so that the RBI should not be required to provide any support to the government market borrowing programme and so on. Unfortunately, before the government could consider the suggestions with any seriousness, the country was plunged into political and economic uncertainties due to unfortunate events that unfolded, which finally necessitated initiating a series of liberalization measures.[6]

Under the provisions of the RBI Act, 1934, India's gold reserves were pegged at a fixed price. However, gold prices had risen significantly over the years and there was substantial divergence in the current rate of gold in domestic as well as international markets and the rate at which RBI's gold reserves were valued. As suggested by Malhotra in his August 1990 letter to the finance minister, the government amended Section 33(4) of the RBI Act. This facilitated the revaluation of the gold assets held by the RBI closer to international prices, increasing the flexibility in the use of gold reserves. The first such revaluation took place on 17 October 1990. Further, the RBI decided to revalue the gold holdings at the end of each month based on the average daily London market prices during the month, keeping a margin of 10 per cent. This change to market-based valuation of gold helped to reflect the appropriate value of gold reserves over time, giving the RBI more flexibility in dealing with multilateral agencies like the IMF and the World Bank.

[6]Ibid. 67–9.

In early 1990, Malhotra decided to expand the RBI's supervision to DFIs and other financial intermediaries. So far, the RBI had been undertaking the supervision of commercial banks only. As such, it was a break from the past, although a necessary step in the right direction. In reply to the government's queries in this regard, he mentioned that the RBI's objective was broadly to monitor and oversee, within the current legislative framework, the operations of financial institutions as an adjunct to monetary and credit policy. The role of the RBI in relation to financial institutions has to be seen essentially in terms of the need for a macro perspective of monetary and credit policy, assessing the quality of assets of the financial system and improving coordination between banks and financial institutions. To further clarify the issues raised, the RBI made it clear that its intention was to establish a monitoring system that served its purpose without interfering with the functional autonomy of the institutions or with the coordinating roles of apex institutions. This move paved the way for the RBI's oversight of the entire financial system in the country in years to come.

Due to growing differences between the finance ministry and the RBI on various issues, Malhotra tendered his resignation on 22 December 1990. Under him, the RBI maintained a strong stance on controlling inflation by moderating fiscal deficits. It also tried to uphold the RBI's autonomy as a monetary authority during a period of increasing financial imprudence. He made successful efforts to make the financial system more flexible and competitive. He implemented a range of reforms in tune with the recommendations of the Chakravarty Committee. He introduced new money market instruments and allowed banks flexibility in fixing interest rates structure. He was ably supported by his deputy, C. Rangarajan, with his sound economic background and analytical mindset, in the area of monetary and credit policy administration.

Even after retirement from the RBI, Malhotra continued to serve the country significantly. A committee was set up in 1993 under the chairmanship of Malhotra to make recommendations for reforms in the insurance sector. The committee submitted its report in 1994, containing several pathbreaking recommendations for reforming the insurance sector. The committee strongly felt that in order to improve the customer services and increase the coverage of insurance, the industry should be opened up to competition. At the same time, it stressed the need to exercise caution as any failure on the part of the new players could ruin the public confidence in the industry. Many of the recommendations have been implemented by the government in the years ahead. The Insurance Regulatory and Development Agency Act (IRDA), 1999, was passed and the IRDA was set up as a statutory body in April 2000. As a result of the committee's recommendations, insurance sector was thrown open for private investment.

Malhotra's wife, Anna, was India's first female IAS officer and chairperson of the Jawaharlal Nehru Port Trust during her last assignment. Malhotra passed away on 29 April 1997.

18

S. Venkitaramanan

S. Venkitaramanan was the eighteenth governor of the RBI. He held this post from 22 December 1990 to 22 December 1992. Venkitaramanan was born on 28 January 1931 in Nagercoil, Tamil Nadu. He holds a master's degree in physics from University College, Thiruvananthapuram, and a master's degree in industrial administration from Carnegie Mellon University, USA. Venkitaramanan was a member of the IAS. He had served as finance secretary to the central government and advisor to the government of Karnataka before he was appointed governor of the RBI.

The year 1990 was full of political uncertainty. Saddam Hussein had invaded Kuwait, and oil prices were soaring. R.N. Malhotra had resigned in the wake of his increasing differences with the Chandrashekhar government. It fell to Venkitaramanan to handle the crisis. He had served as Union finance secretary and was widely held responsible as the man who had steered India towards the financial crisis. He had come up with the idea of the RBI automatically financing the government's deficit through ad hoc treasury bills, perhaps underestimating the skill with which the political class could manipulate bureaucrats and the institutions they ran. Fortunately, he rose to the occasion and his performance as the RBI governor more than compensated for his mistakes as the finance secretary.

When Venkitaramanan assumed charge of the RBI, he was disappointed to find that there was no exact information as to exactly how much foreign exchange India had in its reserves. Public-sector banks kept at least $2 billion as undisclosed reserves in their overseas branches. Only five or six people knew about them: the governor of the RBI, a deputy governor, the finance secretary, the chief economic advisor and the joint secretary in charge of external finance. Rajiv Gandhi had been wary of going to the IMF for assistance, and so this secret reserve was used. The $2 billion that the SBI had borrowed for oil imports was also spent. By December 1990, the SBI branch in New York had barely enough to meet the minimum balance required by the US Federal Reserve. On 1 January 1991, India had just about $1.1 billion in its reserves.

India was flat broke. The situation was dire. It was up to Venkitaramanan to salvage the situation by averting the defaults and steering India away from disaster. Matters became worse when Gandhi withdrew support for the Chandrashekhar government, despite being warned that if the government was toppled, the economic situation would grow dire. It was unforgivably irresponsible, but Gandhi escaped any possible prosecution due to his death in a bomb attack perpetrated by the Liberation Tigers of Tamil Eelam (LTTE) during the campaigning for 1991 general elections.

By mid-February 1991, India was left with just enough foreign exchange to meet two weeks of imports as opposed to the stipulated three weeks. Further, it had become clear to Chandrashekhar's caretaker government that India had exhausted all possible resources to arrange for dollars. The only course left for the government to salvage the situation and redeem its prestige in international fora was to mortgage some of its gold for foreign exchange. Prime Minister Chandrashekhar made the courageous decision of allowing gold to be pledged. Venkitaramanan was in charge of supervising the shipment of gold. A total of 48 tonnes of gold was shipped to the Bank of England in four tranches in almost complete secrecy. However, a press reporter from the *Indian Express* got wind of the operation. The story broke on 7 July 1991, creating a huge scandal and another headache for the newly elected P.V. Narasimha Rao government and the governor of the RBI.

The crisis Venkitaramanan inherited was due to the very loose fiscal policies during 1985–90. For those five years, the then governor Malhotra had repeatedly warned the government about the deteriorating fiscal situation. He had tried to alert the government in time to approach the multilateral agencies for emergency funding. Nobody had either the time or the inclination to bother about the situation, considering the explosive political situation prevailing. V.P. Singh had decided to approach the IMF for funds as soon as he took over as the prime minister in November 1989. However, the file never reached him. It is said that the finance ministry miscalculated the gravity of the situation and the papers did not move in time. As a result, India was on the brink of a major default.

In June 1991, the P.V. Narasimha Rao government came to power with Manmohan Singh as the finance minister. The two of them took charge and Venkitaramanan's duties were curtailed thereafter. Just as he was beginning to enjoy his job, a huge scandal involving the stock markets and banks stunned the entire country, including the RBI and the government.

In 1992, a journalist exposed a scam involving thousands of crores worth of government securities and public-sector bonds. The scam involved a couple of stockbrokers, some well-known Indian banks, a couple of foreign banks and the National Housing Bank as participants. The scam, which broke through a news report in April 1992, involved siphoning off of about ₹5,000 crore from the financial system through a nexus between stockbrokers and senior executives of nationalized banks. It exposed weaknesses in market regulation and securities settlement practices and highlighted serious technological gaps. What caused this was that the public-sector banks were unhappy that they had to rely only on interest as income. In 1987, they were permitted to invest 5 per cent of their incremental deposits in the stock market. The RBI was opposed to the move but could do nothing. In 1991, the government allowed them to invest 5 per cent of total deposits instead of incremental deposits as part of its liberalization policy. Y.V. Reddy was then a joint secretary to the finance ministry who would later become the governor of the RBI. He had vehemently opposed the move considering the inherent dangers involved. However, he was overruled, as the government wanted to give a boost to the stock markets which needed big money and the obvious source of funds was banks.

Harshad Mehta, a share broker on the Bombay Stock Exchange, wanted to invest in a big way in the markets and had zeroed in on banks to raise the resources. But he had to find a way to tap into the banks. He realized that the internal control systems in banks were poor and there was always a substantial time gap in the date of dealing in securities and the actual delivery of the securities. Through a clever mix of fraud and corruption, he got his hands on thousands of crores worth of securities and started manipulating the market by using bank receipts (that were sometimes fake) to raise money against securities he did not own. He single-handedly took the market to dizzying heights. People started calling him 'the big bull'. He was followed by other brokers as well. In a way, brokers were shorting the bond market and going long on stocks. This reflected weaknesses in the internal governance practices in the banks. When the scam was exposed in the newspapers, the markets crashed. It shook the whole nation, including agencies like RBI and the Securities and Exchange Board of India (SEBI). It was alleged that if the RBI had been more vigilant, the scam might not have happened. The RBI's methods of operations were too primitive and plagued with loopholes, making it easy for people like Harshad Mehta to manipulate the systems. In a matter of 13 months between April 1991 and May 1992, Mehta and his co-conspirators had successfully diverted around ₹5,000 crore from the banking system.

The Bombay Stock Exchange witnessed unprecedented bullishness and the Sensex reached a record 4,500 in May 1992 from a low of 1,000 in April 1991. Everyone thought it was because of liberalization and reforms, and even the government was enjoying the bullishness. Sucheta Dalal, an editor at the *Times of India*, leaked the story to the media. The realization struck that the market bullishness was actually due to the tainted money being invested in the market by Harshad Mehta and his cronies. It was termed as the biggest scam of the century and was investigated by the JPC, the RBI, the Central Bureau of Investigation (CBI), etc.

At the insistence of the government, the RBI set up a committee with the deputy governor R. Janakiraman as chairman on 30 April 1992. The committee was to investigate the irregularities in funds management by commercial banks and financial institutions, particularly in their dealings in government securities, public-sector bonds, UTI units and similar instruments. The committee submitted three reports dated 31 May, 5 July and 23 August 1992. It identified serious deficiencies in the functioning of banks and financial institutions involved, and the absence of necessary internal control in various functions. The committee made a series of recommendations to strengthen the system. The government and the RBI moved swiftly with a single-minded pursuit of restoring confidence in the Indian financial system within the country and internationally. One of the measures was strengthening the SEBI.

Venkitaramanan was summoned by the JPC. His response was that the RBI had done its duty by issuing guidelines to banks over do's and don't's in their investment operations and that the senior officers of the banks were responsible for the micromanagement of the banks. His contention was that it was the SEBI that was in charge of the stock markets, not the RBI. He further contended that though the RBI was not directly involved with the stock markets, it was the RBI that had detected the scam and had alerted the others, so on and so forth. The committee was not convinced but let the matter rest there. Negligence by the RBI and corruption in the banks were regarded as the main reasons for the scam. The propriety of Venkitaramanan was called into question. After all, it was he who was presiding over the rotten system. However, Finance Minister Manmohan Singh publicly certified Venkitaramanan's innocence, and told *India Today* that he understood 'the anger of the common man'.[1]

Heads rolled. The government nearly collapsed. New legislation was enacted and the most modern payments and settlements system was installed in the RBI. Most importantly, it forced India to adopt the practice of having a repo or repurchase rate, a practice common in countries with advanced financial markets. But it is astonishing to think of the RBI's single-entry ledgers of banks' bond deals and its cluelessness of what was going on. Managers were taken for a ride by smarter multinational banks. The episode also led to the strengthening of the SEBI and a much tighter watch on foreign banks because they had been the ringleaders in the whole affair. There was a renewed effort to cut the Bombay Stock Exchange down to size by setting up and patronizing the National Stock Exchange. As T.C.A. Srinivasa Raghavan writes, India always needs a major crisis for something good to emerge.[2]

[1]Shankar Aiyar, V. and Shefali Rekhi, 'Securities Scam: After Five Years, ₹12,500 Crore Rip-Off Still Remains Unresolved', *India Today*, 31 May 1997. , http://bit.ly/3ILbPGZ. Accessed on 2 February 2023.

[2]Srinivasa Raghavan, T.C.A., *Dialogue of the Deaf: The Government and the RBI*, Tranquebar Press, 2017, pp. 147–51.

The reforms of 1991 changed the relationship between the governors and the media. Before 1991, the governors avoided the media and the media left them alone. However, after 1991, RBI governors began to court media under the guise of *communicating the markets* and were successful in diverting the media attention towards themselves. Earlier no one bothered to ask whether a governor was successful, but it is now the norm. In one article, Srinivasa Raghavan considers the names of various governors from this point of view. In that article, he includes S. Venkitaramanan as one of the successful governors who saved India from the ignominy of debt default during the critical phase between December 1990 and July 1991, and he rues the fact that Mr Venkitaramanan has been largely forgotten.[3]

---

[3]Srinivasa Raghavan, T.C.A., 'Guess Who Has Been the Best Governor at the RBI?', *Rediff.com,* 16 November 2016. , http://bit.ly/3YTBin4. Accessed 1 February 2023.

19

C. Rangarajan

Dr Chakravarthi Rangarajan was the nineteenth governor of the RBI. He held the post of governor from 22 December 1992 to 21 November 1997.

Unlike his predecessors, Rangarajan came from an academic background instead of a bureaucratic one. He was born on 5 January 1932 and studied at National College, Trichy, from 1947 to 1949. He studied commerce at Loyola College, University of Madras, and was a contemporary of T.N. Srinivasan, who chaired the Department of Economics at Yale University, USA. He completed his doctorate in economics from the University of Pennsylvania, USA, in 1964, where his thesis was titled 'Variability of Demand Deposits'. Rangarajan taught at several prestigious institutions including the Wharton School, University of Pennsylvania, USA; Stern School of Business, New York University, USA, and IIMA, India's premier business school. He was also the chancellor of the University of Hyderabad. He is the founding chairman of the C.R. Rao Advanced Institute of Mathematics, Statistics and Computer Science as well as the Madras School of Economics, Chennai.

From 1992 to 1997, Rangarajan guided the country through a comprehensive programme of economic liberalization and reforms. During his tenure as the governor, he initiated widespread reforms in India's financial and monetary sector, including the current account convertibility of the rupee. In his term as the governor, the RBI was heavily involved in creating a comprehensive set of measures to strengthen and improve the competitive efficiency of the financial sector. New institutions and instruments were introduced; changes in exchange-rate management culminated in the establishment of a unified exchange rate. The RBI and the government signed a memorandum capping the automatic finance provided by the RBI to the government in the form of ad-hoc treasury bills. This ended the four-decade practice of automatic monetization of the fiscal deficit.

Rangarajan has arguably been the most successful governor in the history of the RBI. The sheer number and variety of reforms that he introduced in his tenure allowed him to leave an indelible mark on every area of the economy that falls within the RBI's vast purview, including monetary policy, banking, corporate finance, foreign exchange and the capital markets. For 10 years before his appointment as governor, he served as the deputy governor of the RBI, where he was universally well regarded and admired for his approachability and the clarity of his thoughts. Rangarajan groomed noteworthy successors like Y.V. Reddy and achieved what none of his predecessors easily could: greater autonomy for the RBI.

By the early 1990s, the exchange rate had become central to the management of the external sector as the government wanted to eliminate various trade-related restrictions. In 1991, the Committee on Balance of Payments was formed. It was chaired by Rangarajan. The committee submitted its interim report in February 1992 and final report in April 1993. It recommended the introduction of a liberalized exchange rate management system. This system was introduced in 1992 after extensive discussions between the government and the RBI. It was part of other measures geared at liberalizing the Indian economy. Apart from providing a boost to exports, it aimed at greater economic efficiency. The

Rangarajan Committee emphasized that to achieve the full benefit of integrating the Indian economy with the world economic system, the country had to move step by step towards full convertibility of current account transactions, keeping in view the developments in the macroeconomic situation and the world trading environment. On 1 March 1993, a unified exchange rate was introduced, wherein the exchange rate was determined by demand and supply in the Indian foreign-exchange market. The committee made wide-ranging recommendations on various aspects of India's balance of payments, and a number of its recommendations formed inputs for the policy decisions of that period.

Rangarajan was an able leader who rolled with the punches. The Harshad Mehta scam broke out in April 1992, under the tenure of S. Venkitaramanan, but the fallout was dealt with largely by Rangarajan over the next few years. The scam had taken the country by surprise; though the kingpin was Harshad Mehta, a stockbroker at the Bombay Stock Exchange, the true ringleaders were the multinational banks involved who had taken advantage of lack of internal controls and the primitive recordkeeping systems for government securities in banks. In *Dialogue of the Deaf*, T.C.A. Srinivasa Raghavan writes that the RBI 'went into overdrive' after the scam. Over the next few years, its 'swift and comprehensive' response succeeded in introducing the best practices to supervise the financial sector. He credits this success to Rangarajan, who oversaw the effort.[1]

The RBI, under Rangarajan, made strides towards growth and adapted to the financial needs of the day. In the wake of the Harshad Mehta scam, the RBI introduced new supervision norms over banks, and shifted focus to liquidity and management. The CRR and SLR were reduced to increase the lendable resources of

---

[1]Srinivasa Raghavan, T.C.A., *Dialogue of the Deaf: The Government and the RBI*, Tranquebar Press, 2017, p. 150.

the banks and allow them to determine the rate of interest. Branch licensing was liberalized and banks were given the freedom to open branches where they chose in pursuit of their commercial interests. Prudential norms were introduced, making banks more transparent about their balance sheets and more conscious of the quality of lending. Furthermore, in January 1993, Rangarajan announced the entry of 10 new private-sector banks (including HDFC Bank, ICICI Bank and IndusInd Bank). He also worked towards the technological improvement and organizational restructuring of Indian banks. A new committee of the Central Board of the RBI known as the Board for Financial Supervision (BFS) was created to oversee the supervisory functions. Certain powers that the RBI earlier exercised through its DBOD were now assigned to the BFS.

These measures, along with other measures taken by the government, resulted in improvement in foreign-exchange reserves, lower inflation, lower fiscal deficit and accelerated growth. The FERA was replaced by the FEMA. Foreign institutional investors were allowed to invest in capital markets. The NRIs were allowed to invest in local currency deposits and also in real estate, which resulted in an inflow of much-needed foreign exchange and led to an improvement in India's balance of payments position. The rupee was made convertible in current account transactions.

One of the most important and significant events in the history of the RBI took place in September 1994. The Government of India signed an agreement with the RBI to end the automatic monetization of fiscal deficit by the issue of ad hoc treasury bills, thereby giving the RBI more flexibility in managing the monetary policy. It was agreed that the automatic monetization of the fiscal deficit would be phased out over a period of three years, that is, by 1997–98. Instead of ad hoc treasury bills, the RBI agreed to provide 'ways and means advances' to the government to manage temporary mismatches in its cash flows. The RBI also made available the option of debt funding through 'market sources' such as debt mutual funds, which were allowed to invest in treasury bonds.

What was the significance of this agreement between the government and the RBI? It paved the way for the passing of the FRBM, 2003, which capped the fiscal deficit of the government at a certain percentage of the GDP. From the layperson's perspective, it is akin to the subordinate getting the boss to sign an agreement promising to be more financially prudent and disciplined. Rather than looking to the RBI to fund its ever-increasing expenditure by printing more notes, the government would now have to raise its revenue through other means. The impact of this agreement has echoed through the last 20 years and can be seen in measures aimed at formalizing the economy and increasing revenues to the exchequer. Some examples are the introduction of the Goods and Services Tax (GST), demonetization and the Pradhan Mantri Jan-Dhan Yojana; other examples include amendments to the Benami Transactions (Prohibition) Act, reduction in diversion of subsidies by introducing the Direct Benefit Transfer (whereby the subsidies are directly credited to the accounts of the beneficiaries) and reforms in the food ration system.

Rangarajan was part of policy-making at the RBI for 10 years before becoming the governor and made invaluable contributions to multiple fiscal review committees under successive governments. He wrote the lion's share of the Sukhamoy Chakravarty Committee report, which undertook a comprehensive review of India's monetary system and its interface with fiscal policy, especially its relationship with debt financing and public debt management. The committee was established in 1982, when Dr Manmohan Singh was the governor of the RBI. It submitted its report in 1985, by which time Singh had moved to the Planning Commission. The report was exhaustive, and a virtual blueprint for India's monetary and economic policies for decades to come. In *Dialogue of the Deaf*, Srinivasa Raghavan writes that the RBI owes Rangarajan and S.S. Tarapore 'an immense debt' for the groundwork they laid between 1986 and 1996 for India's future reforms.[2]

Rangarajan was a thoughtful and articulate leader and felt strongly that monetary policy could not be separated from fiscal policy. In 1988, he delivered the presidential address at the annual conference of the Indian Economic Association, where he spoke about the close link between fiscal and monetary policies. The growing budgetary deficit, which was absorbed by the RBI, highlighted the link between fiscal and monetary policies as well as the need for close coordination between the two. In 1997, he expounded further on how price stability was the most important objective of monetary policy in an interview with *Business Today*:

> Price stability is not an end in itself, but a means to ensure sustained economic growth. It achieves a number of things: it promotes savings, prevents the diversion of investment into speculative channels, and sharpens our export competitiveness. In addition, there is a social dimension to price stability. It protects people who have no hedge against inflation. For these reasons, we regard price stability as the most important objective of monetary policy. Stable prices facilitate, not inhibit, growth.[3]

His articulation of the objectives of monetary policy has guided subsequent governors of the RBI. These objectives, according to Rangarajan, cannot be different from the overall objectives of economic policy in India: first, to maintain a reasonable degree of price stability and second, to help accelerate the rate of economic

---

[2]Ibid. 31.

[3]'Price Stability is the Most Important Objective', *Business Today*, 22 December 1997, http://bit.ly/3lOooYW. Accessed on 22 February 2023.

growth.[4] This paradigm shift is reflected in the 'big bang' monetary policy that Rangarajan announced in April 1997, when the future of the Indian government was shrouded in uncertainty. The key feature of this policy was the RBI moving away from micro-regulation to macro-regulation, leaving banks free to do largely as they wished within the parameters established by the RBI.

The incident also asserted the autonomy of the RBI. Rangarajan was clear on what autonomy meant to him: He felt that the institutional arrangement that had evolved gave the RBI sufficient freedom to pursue policy as it saw fit. There was no doubt that in a parliamentary democracy, there needed to be continuous cooperation between the governor of the RBI and the finance minister, as the latter was answerable to Parliament for his economic policy. But Rangarajan saw this effort as harmonious, analogous to musicians in a symphony orchestra. Different musicians in a symphony play different notes at the same time, and they blend to produce beautiful music: There was no need for fiscal and monetary policy to be any different.

However, the two could not run at cross-purposes. While this coordination was desirable, it was necessary for the monetary authority to have institutional autonomy and not be burdened with functions that conflicted with its central objective. This autonomy did not guarantee a rosy future: only that the RBI could pursue a consistent monetary policy over a long time. Rangarajan stressed the importance of 'constrained discretion' in monetary policy: He exhorted central banks to be transparent with their objectives and strategies, giving banks the freedom to choose the timing and nature of their actions. This was the autonomy to which central banks should aspire.

---

[4]Rangarajan, C. 'Monetary Policy in a Developing Economy—The Indian Experience', *Twenty K.R. Narayanan Orations: Essays by Eminent Persons on the Rapidly Transforming Indian Economy*, 1st ed., Raghbendra Jha (ed.), Australia, ANU Press, 2021, pp. 87–102. DOI: 10.2307/j.ctv1prsr3r.14.

The balance between cooperation and independence is difficult to strike, yet Rangarajan managed it with aplomb. He was firm on the autonomy of the RBI, yet maintained harmonious relationships where other governors of the RBI had failed. Rangarajan prevailed upon Finance Minister Manmohan Singh to enter an agreement with the RBI, putting an end to the practice of ad hoc treasury bills. He was also highly regarded by his fellow bankers. Y.V. Reddy described him as 'formidable' and spoke with admiration of his vision and intellect.[5] Reddy praised Rangarajan's academic background and his professorial nature in dealings with functionaries and bankers. His academic background grounded him and helped him develop and articulate a long-term vision of India's future. Former deputy governor of the RBI, Usha Thorat, also spoke of Rangarajan's deep understanding of theory and the confidence that flowed from his understanding. She gave the example of liberalization of gold to demonstrate the courage of his conviction. Where critics had predicted it would fritter away the country's forex reserves, Rangarajan knew that it would instead kill the hawala market.

Perhaps the most impressive praise came from K.R. Narayanan, former president of India, who had this to say about Rangarajan in 2001:

> Hailed as one of the chief architects of India's monetary policy for several years, Dr Rangarajan during his long and distinguished career, particularly during his association with the Reserve Bank of India as deputy governor and subsequently as governor, devised a monetary policy which would facilitate growth and ensure price stability. Most of the measures such as simplification and deregulation of interest rate structure, policy formulations for improving

---

[5]Reddy, Y.V., *Advice and Dissent: My Life in Public Service*, Harper Collins, 2018, pp. 145–7.

> lendable resources of banks, upgradations of the information technologies and introduction of competition in the financial system, have contributed to lay down the foundation of a monetary policy to further strengthen India's new economic environment. While doing so, Dr Rangarajan has proved that in developing countries growth of the economy and price stability can be appropriately blended. New economic policies must not only ensure prosperity and growth, these must also serve other defined goals for the society as a whole. As a moving force behind the liberalisation of our economy and as an active player and economic strategist for building up a dynamic economy, Dr Rangarajan's contributions have become significant. I am sure the range of ideas, the depth of understanding and the wide experience of Dr Rangarajan will be of importance for all developing countries grappling with the emerging realities of liberalisation and financial reforms.[6]

Rangarajan has been honoured with many awards over the course of his illustrious career, including the Padma Vibhushan (2002) and the P.C. Mahalanobis Lifetime Achievement Award for Contribution to Official Statistics (2020) by the Ministry of Statistics and Programme Implementation. He has worked on papers on topics including price behaviour, capital spending, export fluctuation, corporate planning and corporate investment. Rangarajan was a member of the Planning Commission and had also been a member of the Rajya Sabha. He is the former chairman of the prime minister's economic advisory council. While serving as the governor of Andhra Pradesh, he also held additional charge

[6]Narayanan, K.R. '2001 K.R. Narayanan Oration', *Twenty K.R. Narayanan Orations: Essays by Eminent Persons on the Rapidly Transforming Indian Economy*, 1st ed., Raghbendra Jha (ed.), Australia, ANU Press, 2021, pp. 85–6. DOI: 10.2307/j.ctv1prsr3r.13.

as governor of Odisha from 1998 to 1999 and as governor of Tamil Nadu from 2001 to 2002. Presently, he is chairman of the Madras School of Economics, Chennai.

20

Bimal Jalan

Dr Bimal Jalan was the twentieth governor of the RBI. He held office for two successive terms from 22 November 1997 to 21 November 2002, and from 22 November 2002 to 21 November 2004. He succeeded Dr C. Rangarajan and is considered one of India's most successful central bankers.

Jalan was born and raised in Kolkata. He studied at Presidency University and later attended Universities of Cambridge and Oxford. He held several administrative and advisory positions in the government of India before becoming the governor of the RBI. He was chief economic advisor in the 1980s, banking secretary from 1985 to 1989 and finance secretary between January 1991 and September 1992. Jalan was also president of the governing body of the National Council of Applied Economic Research (NCAER) in New Delhi, India's first independent economic policy institute. He has served as the executive director, representing India on the boards of the IMF and the World Bank. He was the chairman of the economic advisory council to the prime minister prior to being appointed as governor.

Jalan took over the reins of governorship from Rangarajan on 22 November 1997, when the country was going through political turmoil. There was no stable government at the Centre and the Asian financial crisis was at its peak. Consequently, there was no possibility of discussing and drafting policy guidelines with the

Central government. Asian countries like Thailand and Indonesia were badly affected and had to devalue their currencies. Jalan received great acclaim for preventing the crisis from affecting India, which had only recently recovered from the balance of payments problem.

In 1998, the National Democratic Alliance formed a government with Atal Bihari Vajpayee as prime minister and Yashwant Sinha as finance minister. As is customary, the governor of the RBI called on the new finance minister. Jalan surprised Sinha by offering to tender his resignation as he had been appointed by the previous Congress government. Sinha was taken aback but assured Jalan that the new government had full faith in his leadership of the RBI and refused to accept his resignation. This gesture reflected both Jalan's sense of propriety and his own confidence in his abilities. These abilities would serve him well: The early years of his tenure were marked by both a string of international crises and Jalan's steady hand guiding India through stormy seas.

Jalan excelled at crisis management. Building up on the reforms initiated by Rangarajan, he initiated a slew of measures to bring India on the path of sustained growth. Jalan understood one thing with greater clarity than any other governor has before or since: For investment to revive, money must not cost too much and certainly not as much as it did in India then. He accelerated the process of bringing down interest rates that Rangarajan had begun.

In May 1998, India undertook nuclear weapons testing, to the consternation of the world. Western powers, such as the USA, UK and Germany, announced severe economic sanctions on India. The markets reacted badly and went down by nearly 20 per cent. The rupee kept on sliding against major currencies: In just two months, India's foreign currency reserves went down by \$2.5 billion. Approaching the IMF or the World Bank to seek support was not an option. This was a difficult situation and needed a tough response. The government and the RBI asked the SBI to float Resurgent India Bonds to garner funds from NRIs and the persons of Indian origin (PIOs). The rate of interest was kept significantly higher at 7.75 per cent per annum for five years. Due to a sense of patriotism, attractive interest rate and confidence in the Indian economy, the NRI and PIO communities responded wholeheartedly to the issue of bonds. Instead of the expected $2 billion, the SBI collected $4 billion over a much shorter period than anticipated.

The success of these bonds raised confidence in the government and the RBI. The latter undertook coordinated action such as raising the repo rate and hiking the CRR. The rupee soon stopped sliding, stabilized and continued to remain stable for a considerable time. However, when oil prices started to rise in 1999, the rupee started weakening. To stem the fall, Jalan asked oil companies to buy the dollars needed for purchase of oil directly from the RBI rather than from the markets. This effectively stabilized the foreign-exchange market. Several measures were announced to deepen the call money market and the repo mechanism.

Jalan saw the need for reforms and, in 1997, he invited M. Narasimham, former governor and chairman of the first Narasimham Committee on financial reforms, to prepare a comprehensive review of the reforms till that time and chart out a course to strengthen the banking sector. The Narasimham Committee-II submitted its report to the government in April 1998. It suggested more autonomy to public-sector banks, delinking ownership of banks and their regulation, setting aside appropriate sums for non-performing assets (NPAs), introduction of minimum capital adequacy norms, improving risk management systems, etc. The RBI not only accepted the recommendations but also announced a new asset-and-liability management system to be followed by banks. The liquidity adjustment facility was introduced, and it was announced that banks would have to achieve a capital adequacy ratio of 9 per cent. Jalan introduced the 'multiple indicator approach' to manage liquidity. These measures have stood the test of time and continue to be relevant even today.

The dot-com bubble burst in 2001, and oil prices began to rise once again. Accordingly, foreign-exchange reserves began to decline. The RBI worked ably with the government and the SBI to raise foreign exchange by issuing India Millennium Deposit Bonds. Once again, the expected inflow of $2 billion was far exceeded, and a total of $5.5 billion was raised. The foreign-exchange reserves improved further due to increasing service exports bringing in dollars.

Jalan's troubles did not end there. After the announcement of the 2001–02 Budget, there was unusual buoyancy in stocks of certain companies dealt in by the broker Ketan Parekh. Investigations by the SEBI revealed that certain banks, both private and cooperative, had funded Ketan Parekh's market exposures. Two prominent banks were Madhavpura Mercantile Cooperative Bank, Ahmedabad, and Global Trust Bank, Secunderabad. After the scam was exposed, both these banks were in trouble, and Jalan immediately took preventive measures to curb the cascading fallout. Madhavpura Bank was liquidated and Global Trust Bank was merged with the OBC. Prudential norms for income recognition and asset classification were extended to cooperative banks as well; severe restrictions were imposed on lending against shares and stocks. These measures are still followed today with much tighter regulation.

Jalan's tenure saw the FRBM Bill being tabled by the government in Parliament in December 2000. After it was reviewed by the Standing Committee on Finance, some provisions of the FRBM Bill were diluted and it was passed into an Act in 2003. The RBI initiated measures to bring about transparency in pricing and liquidity in government securities markets.

By 2003, Jalan had presided over one of the longest periods of monetary easing in the RBI's history, and his term had been extended twice. During Jalan's tenure, the monetary policy process was demystified and central bank communications took a perceived shift towards transparency. His stewardship of the RBI is remembered for the numerous measures taken to strengthen the banking sector, establish new institutions and introduce new instruments. It was characterized by the strengthening of the balance of payments and forex position, low inflation and soft interest rates. His career as the RBI governor was at its peak with a falling fiscal deficit, low inflation, stable growth and significant balance of payments surplus. He had ensured that the RBI's balance sheets were strong. At this point of time, Jalan expressed his desire to retire from the RBI, ahead of the end of his term in 2004. Though his request was accepted, the government nominated him to the Rajya Sabha in August 2003, and his service to the nation continued.

Y.V. Reddy, who succeeded Jalan as governor in 2003, has written extensively about Jalan in his memoir. Reddy worked closely with Jalan in different capacities before he became deputy governor, and he describes, with respect and affection, Jalan's informal and cheerful temperament.[1] We learn from Reddy that Jalan was a strategist who grasped complex realities quickly and intuitively. He believed in theory as a tool to perceive reality. He was a problem solver who also sought to prevent problems before they arose, leading to systemic improvements. Contrary to what one might expect, his informal personal style did not hamper his dealings with political and bureaucratic elements: He kept his cards close to his chest and shared information on a need-to-know basis. Reddy credits him with innovation in leadership and unprecedented crisis

---

[1]Reddy, Y.V., *Advice and Dissent: My Life in Public Service*, Harper Collins, 2018, pp. 143–4.

management and rues that Jalan remains unappreciated for crises he averted before other people noticed them. T.C.A. Srinivasa Raghavan described Jalan's savviness and how his refusal to explicitly commit to anything served him well in his dealings with politicians and bureaucrats.[2] On 18 August 2003, under the heading 'Farewell the Central Banker', *Hindu Businessline* wrote: 'Truly a "political" economist, a thinking man's economist, a pragmatist and a successful practitioner of central banking profiled.'[3]

He was unencumbered by dogma and ideology, and was pragmatic and focused. He spoke often of his intellectual debt to Mancur Olson, the Swedish institutional economist who did pioneering work on the impact that social and economic conditions had on government policy. He was deeply conscious that public policy affects different sections of society differently.

For all of Jalan's non-committal smoothness, which made him a nightmare for journalists, he was admirably comprehensible in the views that guided his actions. He described the question of the RBI's autonomy as over-stretched, particularly for a developing country like India. When it came to the question of autonomy, it was of utmost importance to him that the government and the RBI arrive at a consensus. Ultimately, whatever the fiscal or economic policy dimensions may be, politics trumped economics. With respect to issues that were difficult to handle, it was critical to have a consultative and collaborative equation between the Bank and the government. There were bound to be minor issues and differences, but communication was essential for the two to work together for national interests.

Reflecting on lessons learnt from his tenure as the RBI governor, Jalan said:

---

[2]Srinivasa Raghavan, T.C.A., *Dialogue of the Deaf: The Government and the RBI*, Tranquebar Press, 2017, pp. 164–5.

[3]'Farewell the Central Banker', *Bimal Jalan*, https://bit.ly/3XWR7Z9. Accessed on 19 January 2023.

> One should not sound pompous but the most important lesson is to keep your feet firmly on the ground. The second lesson is that the consultative process is probably the best method. There are no hard and fast rules that work all the time. So, you should have an open mind and take decisions after due consultation with others. And the third lesson, I would say is, don't go by the established fad of the day in terms of economic policy. All the talk about fixed exchange rate, flexible exchange rate, appreciating exchange rate, capital account convertibility and so on are very good as principles. But when the chips are down, the country has to make its own decisions. In making these decisions the most important thing is to keep the country's interest in view rather than what others are saying.[4]

Jalan continued to serve the country long after retiring from the RBI. In November 2018, he chaired the expert committee to review the extant economic capital framework of the RBI that was constituted by the RBI and the Government of India. The committee submitted its report in August 2019 to the then governor of the RBI, Urjit Patel. The committee's recommendations were based on the consideration of the role of central banks' financial resilience, cross-country practices, statutory provisions, the impact of the RBI's public-policy mandate and operating environment on its balance sheet and the risks involved. It was guided by the fact that the RBI forms the primary bulwark for monetary, financial and external stability. Therefore, the resilience of the RBI needs to be commensurate with its public-policy objectives and must be maintained above the level of peer central banks, as would be expected of a central bank of one of the fastest growing large economies of the world. The far-reaching recommendations made

[4]Bandyopadhyay, Tamal, "'My Departure Was Not Thrust Upon Me'", *Business Standard*, 3 September 2003.

by the committee resolved the long-standing dispute between the government and the RBI over the amount of dividend to be transferred by the RBI to the government every year.

Jalan was chairman of the ISI from 1999 to 2002. He has also chaired a number of distinguished academic institutions such as the Indira Gandhi Institute of Development Research, NCAER and the Institute of Economic Growth.

TRIVIA

1. Y.V. Reddy succeeded Bimal Jalan as the governor of the RBI in 2003. Jalan was the governor from 1997 to 2003, while Reddy was the deputy governor from 1996 to 2002. Both Jalan and Reddy were born on 11 August 1941.
2. Major institutions like the IDBI, UTI and Agricultural Refinance Corporation were formed and established during the tenure of P.C. Bhattacharya. The Credit Guarantee Corporation was formed under S. Jagannathan while B.N. Adarkar played a pivotal role in the establishment of the NIBM, Pune. During R.N. Malhotra's tenure, the Indira Gandhi Institute of Development Research was inaugurated and the Discount and Finance House of India and the National Housing Bank were established.
3. H.V.R Iengar was the chairman of the SBI when he was appointed as the governor of the RBI. He was succeeded by P.C. Bhattacharyya as chairman of the SBI. It was sort of a coincidence that when Iengar retired from the RBI as the governor, he was succeeded by P.C. Bhattacharyya once more.
4. Manmohan Singh was the governor of the RBI when Pranab Mukherjee was the finance minister (1982–84). Later, Pranab Mukherjee served as finance minister (2009–12) when Manmohan Singh became the prime minister for the second time.

21

Y.V. Reddy

Dr Yaga Venugopal Reddy was the twenty-first governor of the RBI. He held the post from 6 September 2003 to 5 September 2008. Reddy was born on 17 August 1941 in Kadapa, Andhra Pradesh. He received his master's degree in economics from the University of Madras and completed his doctorate from Osmania University, Hyderabad. Reddy taught at Osmania University before joining the IAS. He spent most of his career in areas of finance and planning. Before being appointed as the governor of the RBI, Reddy was India's executive director on the board of the IMF.

Reddy was not new to the RBI. He was the Bank's deputy governor for six years between 1996 and 2002. Working under Bimal Jalan had given him first-hand experience in the planning and execution of reforms and maintenance of cordial relations with the government. He had seen Jalan's handling of the Asian foreign exchange crisis as well as the stock market scam committed by stockbroker Ketan Parekh and his cronies. Consequently, he was war-ready when he took over as the governor. Reddy was appointed for a full term of five years, a practice almost forgotten by the government since the 1980s. Most governors since 1982 had been initially appointed for either two or three years and had their term extended later, if at all. A five-year appointment must have been a confidence booster and indicated that Reddy would enjoy his tenure relatively free of intervention and marked by autonomy.

When Reddy took over as the governor from Jalan, the economy was in fine fettle. Interest rates were falling, inflation was low, the rupee was stable or appreciating against major currencies and growth was picking up. The only issue was the increasing foreign-exchange reserves. The continued inflow from foreign investors, NRIs and services exports had brought India far from the difficult days of repeated foreign-exchange crises just a decade ago. India was now staring at a substantial surplus that needed to be put to proper use, lest it have an adverse impact on domestic liquidity and stoke inflation. Reddy appointed an internal working group under Usha Thorat, the executive director of the RBI. In its 2003 report, the group advised use of several new monetary instruments.

On the advice of the RBI, the government repaid high-cost foreign currency loans taken out previously ahead of schedule. The Resurgent India Bonds were also paid comfortably. Guidelines permitting industries to raise funds through external commercial borrowings in a calibrated manner were issued in 2004. The same year also saw Moody's Investors Service, a reputed international credit-rating agency, raise India's foreign currency rating to investment grade. This made it easier to raise funds from international markets at a cheaper rate. Buoyed by its comfortable foreign currency reserves position, the RBI permitted corporations to raise foreign currency loans for investment abroad or for investment in joint ventures overseas.

In 2004, the government allowed the RBI to mop up excess liquidity in the system under the Market Stabilization Scheme (MSS). Under the scheme, the RBI would issue securities to mop up excess liquidity on behalf of the government. It was agreed that though the government would bear the interest cost on such securities, it would not use the funds for its own expenditure. It is a testament to Reddy's powers of persuasion that such an agreement was brokered. The scheme was launched on 1 April 2004, giving the RBI a mandate to issue securities up to ₹60,000 crore.

The year 2004 was eventful. The Vajpayee government lost power to the UPA, led by Sonia Gandhi. Manmohan Singh took over as the prime minister of the country and P. Chidambaram was appointed as finance minister. This sudden turn of events created panic in the markets, leading to equities being sold off and loss of foreign capital, to an extent. But Chidambaram was quick to assuage the markets by announcing that the reforms would remain on track. After the new government took over, there were many in the government asking the finance minister and the RBI to utilize the excess reserves for domestic infrastructure development. Even some well-known Western economists had advocated the idea. However, the RBI, first under Jalan and then under Reddy, remained unswayed by the logic put forth. It was economically unsound, and improper besides. Both the governors were against the idea; the foreign exchange, converted to rupees, had already been placed in the market. It was also not up to the RBI to decide how to use those funds. That decision lay primarily with the recipients of the funds. The RBI's resolute refusal to use the forex reserves for domestic infrastructure development would prove to be critical in shielding India from the worst of the American subprime mortgage crisis in 2008.

Reddy's term was marked by external challenges to India's economy that required deft handling. Midway through 2004, international crude oil prices started to rise and inflation began to inch upwards as the prices of other commodities rose. Reddy warned the government and the markets of rising inflation and took measures to tame inflation, such as tightening liquidity by raising the CRR and repo rate. The next year saw the RBI gain the autonomy to fix the CRR and SLR without any limits. Over the course of 2005, the RBI liberalized its policy for foreign banks and allowed them to operate in India more freely. It also allowed Indian banks to increase their presence overseas. The capital adequacy ratio was increased to 9 per cent from the global norm of 8 per cent. Amidst all these changes, Reddy sought to review the state of the economy more frequently and announced a quarterly monetary policy review instead of a biannual one, as was the norm until then.

In 2006, the RBI introduced National Electronic Funds Transfer, a system to revolutionize payments in India. It oversaw the successful redemption of India Millennium Deposit Bonds and temporarily suspended the issue of securities under the MSS due to tight liquidity conditions. Reddy, ahead of the curve, began to tighten monetary policy while inflation was within a manageable limit. It soon became clear that the year's monsoon would be abnormal; inflation began to creep upwards. The RBI sought to maintain price stability and swiftly increased policy rates midway without waiting for the quarterly policy review meeting. The rates were raised five times during 2006. Yet Reddy maintained balance within India even as he strengthened India's external financial position. The RBI liberalized the use of foreign exchange for corporations. It also allowed banks and corporations to raise foreign exchange through external commercial borrowings and other modes. The quota for foreign portfolio investors was raised, thereby liberalizing their investment. Soon, the RBI was dealing with a deluge of foreign exchange.

Reddy's time in office saw the Indian economy experience years of unprecedented growth, coming in at 8 per cent and sometimes even higher than that. Like Rangarajan before him, Reddy's concern was maintaining price stability while not losing momentum in growth. This often put him in a difficult position with Chidambaram, who was eager to maintain a GDP growth rate of 10 per cent or higher and saw the RBI's measures to contain inflation as slowing down growth. The two differed on what policy measures to adopt, and Reddy referred to these differences as 'creative tension'. In his view, it was important to be measured about the RBI's position. There were bound to be conflicts. If there were none, then the RBI was superfluous to the government; conversely, if there were only disagreements, then it was an obnoxious situation.

In January 2007, Standard and Poor's also upgraded India's sovereign rating to investment grade. More foreign exchange flowed in. Worried about inflationary pressures developing in the economy due to excess liquidity, the RBI kept on increasing the CRR and other policy rates. Interbank call rates shot up, sometimes up to 75 per cent. Reddy responded by putting a ceiling of ₹3,000 crore for parking funds with the RBI and asking banks to trade the surplus liquidity in the interbank market. This was called the reverse repo ceiling. Call rates came down to almost zero, and the US dollar traded at ₹40 to the earlier ₹44. By December, inflation had fallen back to a normal 5 per cent, within the RBI's comfort zone.

Since 1955, the RBI had held a 59.7 per cent ownership stake in the SBI. This amounted to a conflict of interest as a regulator's equity was exposed to a regulated entity. Several committees had recommended the transfer of the RBI's stake in the SBI to the government. The move would also enable the RBI to concentrate on its core function as the banking regulator in India. However, the government had dithered over the issue for years, and by June 2007, it was past time to act. The government amended the SBI Act through an ordinance, and the RBI's 59.7 per cent stake was transferred to the government.

Reddy's memoirs are a gripping account of the challenges that come from leading the RBI. He took a measured approach to tensions with the government and the RBI's place in the order of things. His clarity and solidity guided governors before and after him to assert the autonomy of the RBI. In *Advice and Dissent*, he describes the uncertainty around the government in 1997, when the Congress had withdrawn support for the government and the then governor wanted to postpone announcing the policy for a later date when discussions could guarantee the full support of the government. Reddy urged him to announce the annual credit policy, which would come to be known as the big bang policy, on the planned date of 5 May 1997. It would show that the RBI functions apolitically and allow the RBI to push through, in the political vacuum back then, proposals to which the government was unlikely to grant their formal approval. It was necessary that these proposals were ones that the RBI was certain were important for the common good and also unlikely to be reversed by the Indian government. To liven up the atmosphere, he added, 'Sir, autonomy is seldom granted. It has to be grabbed.'[1]

It was clear that Reddy knew his own mind and was not easily cowed down. At the same time, he was pragmatic. He understood that it was important to have a cooperative relationship with the government. In May 2004, less than a year into his tenure as governor, he found himself facing a similar situation as Rangarajan had faced in 1997. The annual policy statement was slated for 18 May 2004, but the UPA government would not be sworn in until after that. Even at the risk of irking the incoming government by not consulting them before announcing the policy, Reddy decided to go ahead and announce it to show that the central bank of the country was in full command and separate from the ruling political party, particularly during periods of political uncertainty. This would reassure the financial markets and also give the RBI a chance to highlight the benign macroeconomic environment, which would provide comfort in a time of change. Still, Reddy was careful to announce a policy that would be acceptable to the

---

[1]Reddy, Y.V., *Advice and Dissent: My Life in Public Service*, Harper Collins, 2018, pp. 135–6.

incoming leadership, and in the end there was no controversy.

It would not always be such smooth sailing. Reddy's relationship with Chidambaram was occasionally tense. A particular bone of contention between the two was the issue of opening up Indian banks to foreign ownership. Reddy was opposed to this policy. Given the ever-shifting political realities that impacted economic policies, Reddy felt that regulating and supervising foreign banks in India would be more difficult than doing the same for domestic banks. His stint as executive director at the IMF had only strengthened these feelings. The literature and case studies on the subject showed that the benefits of the increased presence of foreign banks were uncertain. India's obligations under the World Trade Organization (WTO) did not require it, and Reddy felt that they could not allow themselves to be distracted from the important and painful domestic banking reforms that were still pending. The governance standards in the domestic private-sector banks needed to be improved first. A regulatory framework for bank ownership in general had yet to be developed. The issue of foreign ownership did not arise as a criterion to make banks 'fit and proper'.

Reddy's logic was sound. The thrust of his argument was that in both industrialized and developing countries, the supervisors (here, the RBI) evaluate the benefits and risks of licensing foreign banks in the context of the specific country, according to 'fit and proper' criteria, using guidelines that are judgment-based and evolving. Reddy felt that in India, it was necessary to evaluate the foreign banks on a case-by-case basis while keeping in mind the broader picture, such as domestic banking sector consolidation, India's obligations under the WTO and other considerations. Facing tremendous political pressure to go ahead with the policy, Reddy conveyed to Finance Secretary Rakesh Mohan that he would step down as governor because he could not wholeheartedly support the government's decision. Eventually a compromise was worked out: The government would announce a policy to the desired effect, but the RBI would propose a step-by-step timebound roadmap addressing all the concerns in such a policy. The 2005 Budget speech saw Chidambaram acknowledge the RBI's autonomy in his mention of reforms in the banking sector. He said that most proposals would be implemented by the RBI 'on its own authority'. The required legislative changes would be made 'in consultation with the RBI'.[2] There was no denying the centrality of the RBI in the process.

Reddy differed with Chidambaram on other issues, like the possibility of a Tobin tax and the issue of participatory notes. A Tobin tax is a tax on spot currency conversions. Named after the economist James Tobin, it is meant to penalize short-term currency speculation. It was proposed to financial sector participants as a means of controlling the stability of a country's currency. Today, it is more formally known as a financial transactions tax or, less formally, a Robin Hood tax. Unlike Chidambaram, Reddy was strongly in favour of imposing a Tobin tax and would repeat the call for one in 2011, well after the end of his term in 2008.

The other issue concerned participatory notes, which are often associated with black money. Participatory notes are financial instruments through which overseas investors invest in India without revealing their identity to the regulators. They, therefore, provide a mechanism for round-tripping, or taking money illegally out of India and then investing in India, thereby escaping taxation. In September 2003, the RBI had decided to stop investments by overseas corporate bodies in India to avoid such round-tripping. However, Reddy's attempts to persuade the government to pass such a ban on participatory notes were far from fruitful. Chidambaram strongly felt that the issue of participatory notes

---

[2]'Budget 2005-2006: Speech of P. Chidambaram—Minister of Finance', *Union Government Budget*, https://bit.ly/3EvopHT. Accessed on 1 February 2023.

needed to be settled and, to that end, appointed an expert group chaired by Ashok Lahiri, then-chief economic advisor. A nominee of the RBI was also a member of the group.

The expert group recommended an approach to participatory notes that the RBI considered to be excessively liberal, and the RBI's representative was isolated in the expert group. Consequently, the draft contained the recommendations acceptable to all members of the group but the RBI nominee, who wrote a dissent note. This was what Reddy had hoped to avoid. It would be unprecedented, certainly. But he instructed the RBI nominee not to sign anything unless the RBI's reservations were incorporated in a dissent note. Chidambaram wanted the problem to be settled, and if a dissent note was inevitable, so be it. The report was finally submitted by the chairman of the expert group along with the dissent note by the RBI nominee, which explicitly brought on record the serious concerns of the RBI regarding participatory notes.[3]

Reddy's pragmatism and strength of will could easily have made him obnoxious, but he maintained a sense of humour about his job. Asked about the RBI's independence, he said, 'We are totally free—within the limits set by the government.' On another occasion he remarked, 'The RBI has full autonomy. I have taken the permission of my finance minister to tell you that.'[4]

Reddy advised that a governor has to be quietly confident. He should be neither exuberant nor diffident. He has to often pretend that the RBI is independent; at the same time, he has to ensure not to offend the government. The governor has to keep in mind that the RBI is not equal to the government but has to demonstrate convincingly that the RBI is not subordinate to the government either. Reddy felt that the work of governor is challenging and fascinating at the same time.

---

[3]Ibid. 278–80.

[4]'RBI Independent Within Limits Set by Government, Says Y V Reddy', *Financial Express*, 29 June 2017, https://bit.ly/3Slgd2F. Accessed on 1 February 2023.

Reddy presided over a period of high growth, low inflation, stable rupee and ample foreign-exchange reserves. As governor, Reddy made sure the Indian banks did not get too caught up in the bubble mentality. He banned the use of bank loans for the purchase of raw land, restricted securitizations and derivatives and essentially stopped the off-balance sheet financing. He increased the risk weightages on commercial buildings, shopping mall construction and bank reserve requirements. Reddy is credited for playing a crucial role in framing macroeconomic policies that helped quarantine India from the domino effect of the 1990s Asian financial crisis. He, along with Rangarajan, formulated a course of action to resolve India's balance of payments crisis.

Reddy's work on rural banking is less discussed. His focus was on the common person, and he wanted to revive cooperative banks. Reddy emphasized financial inclusion with the use of information technology. He first used the term 'financial inclusion' in his annual policy statement in April 2005. The concept swiftly gained ground in India and the world, and Reddy continues to be consulted on financial issues by institutions the world over. He delivered the Per Jacobsson Foundation Lecture on 24 June 2012 at the annual meeting of central bank governors in Basel, Switzerland, and spoke on society, economic policies and the financial sector. The core message in his speech was:

> The central banks are expected to ensure trust and confidence in money and finance, and avoid the pitfalls of regulatory capture (capture of regulator by the interests of the regulated), while the common person seeks inclusive finance. Central banks need to preserve space for public policy at the national level consistent with their obligations to the global economy. The financial sector may draw lessons from global coordination in other industries, especially in managing networks. Better regulation warrants effective

> regulation. Consideration of regulation, competition and ownership in an integrated manner, enhanced monitoring of financial market activities and the use of fiscal tools to supplement regulation could be helpful in this regard. Central banks have to ensure that bank managements and the financial sector in general serve the masses, and not merely the elite or the financially active.[5]

Reddy and his work as a banker were universally well regarded and continue to remain so long after he has left office. Joseph Stiglitz, Nobel laureate and professor of economics at Columbia University, USA, said of Reddy: 'If America had a central bank chief like Dr. Y.V. Reddy, the U.S. economy would not have been in such a mess.'[6] Stiglitz was far from the only foreign economist to praise Reddy's sagacity. Stephen Roach, chief economist at Morgan Stanley, described the RBI and Reddy as 'one of India's great stories'. He spoke with admiration of the RBI's fierce independence in the face of political pressure, calling Reddy one of the only two central bankers that sensed the dangers of asset bubbles (the other being Jean-Claude Trichet) and the only one with the courage to act.

Reddy also piqued the interest of journalists. In December 2008, Joe Nocera wrote for the *New York Times* how Reddy helped India avoid a crisis. Bankers had been furious with Reddy when he raised interest rates and risk weights, but admitted later that he saved them. In June 2010, Robert Kuttner wrote an article called 'Ask Dr. Reddy' for *HuffPost Business*. Kuttner had met Reddy at a United Nations conference in 2008, when the financial meltdown had just begun to turn critical. Reddy had shared his fears with him. Kuttner wrote in the piece that Reddy, along with

---

[5] Reddy, Y.V., *Advice and Dissent: My Life in Public Service*, Harper Collins, 2018, pp. 292–3.

[6] NDTV, 'India Didn't Follow Mindless Liberalisation: Joseph Stiglitz', YouTube, 23 December 2008, https://bit.ly/3YEGoUe. Accessed on 19 February 2023.

Richard Koo in Japan and Lord Adair Turner from the UK, was one of three stars that the USA could learn from when it came to regulating the financial sector.

There is no shortage of people who admire Reddy at home. P. Chidambaram called Reddy 'one of the brightest intellectuals living in India today' and also 'the most eminent central banker of the last decade across the world'. He praised the measures Reddy took to prevent and prepare for financial crises in India, saying:

> Venu prepared the country well for the crisis. He recognised that there was an increase in aggregate demand and he took steps on the monetary side with a careful and calibrated increase of repo and reverse repo rates. Then when inflows of foreign capital started increasing, he started the market stabilisation fund for mopping up the resultant liquidity and didn't allow the government to use it.[7]

Usha Thorat, who worked under him for years, observed that there was a difference between Reddy, the deputy governor and Reddy, the governor. He was highly innovative as a deputy because he did not have to deal with the RBI as a whole and could challenge the governor. Yet becoming governor did not change him fundamentally. He remained extremely strategic, and an 'ideas person'. He continued to challenge the way the RBI worked. Raghuram Rajan wrote that Reddy, unlike many of his Western counterparts, did not have to rescue his reputation through a massive bank bailout or through aggressive monetary policy. He kept his reputation 'the old-fashioned central banker way: by just saying no as the economy started partying'.[8]

---

[7]Vageesh, N.S., 'Reddy and Chidambaram: Embrace of the Gladiators', *Hindu Businessline*, 27 January 2011, http://bit.ly/41lAY2b. Accessed on 22 February 2023.

[8]Rajan, Raghuram, 'The Philosophy of Dr Reddy'. *The Indian Express*, 28 April 2013, https://bit.ly/3xAeHQM. Accessed on 19 February 2023.

T.C.A. Srinivasa Raghavan writes that Reddy's prescience stood the country in good stead, and that he has gone down in Indian banking history as one of the best ever RBI governors that the country has seen.

Reddy retired on 5 September 2008 and handed over the charge to D. Subbarao, thus bringing down the curtains on an illustrious period at the RBI. He has written extensively on the Indian economy and financial reforms. He was awarded India's second highest civilian honour, the Padma Vibhushan, in 2010.

22

D. Subbarao

Dr Duvvuri Subbarao took over as the twenty-second governor of the RBI on 5 September 2008 and held on till 4 September 2013. Born in 1949, Subbarao hails from Eluru, a city near Vijayawada, Andhra Pradesh. He holds a BSc (Hons) in physics from IIT Kharagpur and MSc in physics from IIT Kanpur. He completed his doctorate from Andhra University and wrote his thesis on fiscal reforms at the sub-national level. He stood first in the Union Public Service Commission (UPSC) examination and joined the IAS. Subbarao was finance secretary before he was appointed as the governor of the RBI.

Subbarao's initial appointment was for a period of three years. His term was extended for two more years in 2011. Subbarao was involved in initiating fiscal reforms at the state level, and is credited with the financial turnaround of Andhra Pradesh in the late 1990s, when the state had slipped into an unprecedented fiscal crisis. He has written extensively on issues in public finance, decentralization and political economy of reforms.

Subbarao was not the only contender for the post of governor. Y.V. Reddy's term would have been extended, but he was not keen on the idea. Others included Rakesh Mohan and Montek Singh Ahluwalia. Mohan was the deputy governor of the RBI; he had already served for six years and was fully familiar with the RBI's working, making him an excellent choice. Ahluwalia was the deputy chairman of the Planning Commission. Finance Minister P. Chidambaram preferred Subbarao, and so he was appointed after having been interviewed by Chidambaram and Rangarajan.

When Subbarao took charge in 2008, inflation was around 12 per cent but it was showing a downward bias. The economy appeared to be on a strong wicket. There seemed to be no real reason to worry.

That did not last. Barely a fortnight into Subbarao's tenure, the US-based investment bank Lehman Brothers went bankrupt and triggered a global economic downturn. Though the crisis (often compared to the Great Depression) started in the USA, it spread to Europe and other markets, including India. Subbarao was no novice, and coped with the fallout well. His immediate concern was to ensure financial stability.

The RBI and government took immediate action to handle the crisis. The RBI ensured that liquidity did not dry up. The SEBI ensured that the stock markets remained calm and unaffected by the crisis. Chidambaram and Subbarao spoke to the press, assuring them that things were within control and no depositor of any bank would face any difficulty in getting their money. For a few days, the RBI kept a close watch on the entire banking system to ensure that order prevailed. In October alone, the RBI slashed the CRR by 3 per cent to bring it down to 6 per cent, releasing liquidity of ₹1,20,000 crore into the system. Even the repo rate was cut by 1 per cent. Subbarao and the RBI took proactive steps to manage the situation, infuse liquidity in the markets and restore business confidence. The Ministry of Finance and Chidambaram also became very active, taking steps directly that fell within the purview of the RBI. Subbarao was irritated, but having been chosen by Chidambaram, he could do no more than lodge a complaint with Chidambaram.

As it was, they would need to present a united front as another crisis would hit India on 26 November 2008. Terrorists from

Lashkar-e-Taiba attacked multiple locations in Mumbai, including Chhatrapati Shivaji Maharaj Terminus and the Taj Mahal Hotel. The terrorists held hostages at the hotel for nearly three days, a stone's throw away from the RBI headquarters and the Bombay Stock Exchange. Chidambaram ordered the markets to reopen on 28 November in spite of the emergency, wanting to signal to the world that normalcy had returned. With the combined efforts of the SEBI and the RBI, the markets opened on 28 November as desired.

Reducing the CRR by 4 per cent in tranches and repo rate by 1.5 per cent meant that the RBI had released an estimated ₹4,90,000 crore in the system by March 2009. This ensured that no bank faced any liquidity issues, and Subbarao's worries about inflation were also needless as it dropped to almost zero. The RBI had emerged unscathed from one of the worst financial crises in decades. Subbarao must have welcomed the normalcy after finding himself with a crisis on his hands a week into his new appointment, where he was surrounded by RBI staff that was suspicious of him as he had just come from the ministry. Still, normalcy returned and soon Subbarao gained the trust of the RBI staff as well.

After the global recession, Subbarao did not take long to realize that the Indian economy would not remain immune from global developments. Manufacturing growth was slowing, inflation was reaching double digits and stock markets were falling. Many Indian corporations that had made billion-dollar acquisitions abroad were over-leveraged. The rupee was under pressure due to flight of capital, especially by foreign institutional investors. When Subbarao cut the repo rate to stimulate growth in the early months of his tenure, he was criticized by many bankers as inflation, too, was inching up and rate cuts would only accelerate it.

The UPA won the 2009 general elections in India. Manmohan

Singh continued to be the prime minister and Pranab Mukherjee took over as the finance minister. It was widely expected that the government would be more aggressive this time on reforms. While Subbarao mulled over how to unwind the excess liquidity in the system, India had to face another crisis in the form of the worst drought in nearly 40 years. The RBI once again walked a tightrope trying to maintain the momentum of growth while bringing inflation, which had begun to rise again, under control. The RBI began to tighten the loose monetary policy that had followed in the wake of the subprime mortgage crisis. The same year, India bought gold from the IMF, which was selling gold on account of being short on capital. Of the 400 metric tonnes sold by the IMF, India bought half, diversifying its foreign-exchange reserves. This was a far cry from 1991, when India mortgaged its gold to remain financially afloat.

Inflation continued to be an issue throughout 2010. The RBI kept raising policy rates and also kept warning the government about the ballooning fiscal deficit. It had reached 7 per cent in 2009–10 as opposed to the 4 per cent at which the government had agreed to contain it. Mukherjee was uncomfortable with the RBI's stance; the government did not want to slow down the growth or rein in expenditures and investments. Tensions between the government and the RBI began to rise. Usha Thorat's term was not extended despite her exemplary performance as deputy governor and Subbarao's recommendation for her reappointment. The fallout continued. There were jurisdictional disputes between the RBI, SEBI and IRDA as to who would regulate the unit-linked products. Subbarao put up a spirited fight against what he perceived as an affront to the RBI's autonomy and interference in its jurisdiction. Considering the issues involved, the government set up the Financial Stability Development Council (FSDC) for resolving differences among regulators, with the final arbiter being the government. Subbarao objected to this as well. Finally, the government relented and, to allay the RBI's fears of losing autonomy, the governor of the RBI was made the vice-chairman of the council, with the chairman being the finance minister.[1]

In spite of a windfall of almost ₹1,00,000 crore in the form of license fees from the spectrum auction in 2010, the fiscal deficit did not let up. The rising fiscal deficit and imbalances in the economy meant that the economy ran the risk of inflation, as the RBI repeatedly pointed out. It also studied the price situation at a micro level and pointed out the exact causes of price spiral, but the finance ministry still appeared clueless about what policy actions to take. Subbarao was persistent in asking for policy action from the government to rein in the fiscal deficit while he kept increasing the policy rates, which had by now reached pre-2008 levels. In the meantime, Subbarao's term was drawing to an end. He did not want to ask for an extension, and the finance minister did not appear to be keen on granting him one. Finally the prime minister intervened, and Subbarao's term was extended by two years.

Inflation did not show any signs of slowing until the end of 2011. On the other hand, growth decelerated. The RBI and Subbarao were blamed for the growth rate slowing from 9 per cent to 6 per cent and began to ease the tight monetary policy to balance the situation. In 2012, the RBI cut policy rates moderately to spur growth. Subbarao declined the finance minister's request to reduce rates further as the government had not reined in the fiscal deficit. It was also reasonable in his view to sacrifice some short-term growth to contain inflation. The RBI's tightening of monetary policy would hamper growth, but the needs of the silent constituency—the poor who were most affected by inflation—had to be addressed too. Chidambaram, who had resumed the post

---

[1]'RBI Governor Duvvuri Subbarao Says FSDC Must Limit Itself to Coordination', *The Indian Express*, https://bit.ly/3xB5oji. Accessed on 20 February 2023.

of finance minister in July 2012 after Mukherjee resigned to take over as the president of India, declared that growth was as much a challenge as inflation, and said that 'if the government has to walk alone to face the challenge of growth, the government will walk alone'.[2] Tensions between Chidambaram and Subbarao soared. As a consequence, Deputy Governor Subir Gokarn's tenure was not extended despite Subbarao's pleas.

When Subbarao began his term as governor, the rupee stood at ₹44 to a dollar. By the time he retired in 2013, the rupee had fallen to ₹68 to a dollar. His policy had been to allow the rupee to find its own level and intervene only when the markets became too volatile. This hands-off approach from the RBI was to the advantage of currency speculators, who had a field day knowing the RBI would not intervene. The rupee fell dramatically against the dollar during 'taper tantrum'.[3] India's toxic combination of high inflation, fiscal stress and a record current account deficit earned it a place amongst the Fragile Five—the five most vulnerable markets identified by analysts such as Morgan Stanley. The others were South Africa, Turkey, Brazil and Indonesia. While the government blamed external factors for the fall of the rupee, the RBI chose to be objective and reasoned that the rupee's fall was also due to domestic reasons such as the widening current account deficit and fiscal deficit.[4]

In a bid to defend the rupee, Subbarao chose the textbook move of pushing up interest rates instead of signalling to the markets that the RBI's commitment to defend the rupee was credible. At the press conference where Subbarao announced his last monetary policy before his retirement, the outgoing governor

[2]Dasgupta, Ashok, 'We Will "Walk Alone" If Need Be: Chidambaram', *The Hindu*, 30 October 2012, https://bit.ly/41bDmZa. Accessed on 20 February 2023.

[3]Taper tantrum was the investors' immediate reaction after the US Federal Reserve announced that it would reduce its asset purchases in 2013.

[4]Subbarao, Duvvuri, *Who Moved My Interest Rate: Leading the Reserve Bank through Five Turbulent Years*, Penguin, 2016, pp. 423–5.

was asked by a journalist if the measures to defend the rupee would be withdrawn. His answer was that liquidity restrictions would be withdrawn once the exchange rate stabilized. He added that he was aware of the impact that tight liquidity could have on growth. It is reflective of the RBI governor's tremendous influence that when this statement was misinterpreted by traders as meaning that the RBI was not sufficiently committed to defending the rupee, the rupee sank again. Subbarao used a teleconference the next day as a chance to correct this misinterpretation. Replying to a related question, he reiterated the RBI's commitment to stabilizing the rupee and asserted that the benefits of a stable rupee, in the given context, outweighed the benefits of growth. It was essentially what he had said the day before. Only this time, he said it the way markets wanted to hear it, correcting for nuance and making an effort to sound more 'alpha male', as he described it. Saying that the restrictions would not be withdrawn until there was firm evidence that the rupee had stabilized instead of saying that they would be withdrawn when the rupee was stable was what was needed. The rupee recovered soon.[5]

Subbarao's tenure saw relations between the RBI and the government sour. His memoir provides ample examples of disagreements with both Mukherjee and Chidambaram as well as Subbarao's defense of the RBI's authority and autonomy. For instance, Mukherjee's unilateral declaration that new banking licenses would be issued flew in the face of Subbarao's assertion that there was no need for new banks or new licenses. This was firmly the RBI's decision, as the finance ministry is not a licensing authority. Another example is when Chidambaram constituted a liquidity management committee with the finance secretary as chairman. He then sought the RBI's representation on that committee but was declined. Subbarao was upset about

---

[5]Ibid. 545–50.

Chidambaram stepping into what was clearly RBI turf. These revelations hold value in our current context as well. In a highly integrated world economy, foreign investors attach value to the credibility and independence of a central bank. The strength of official currency comes from trust in this bank, emphasizes Subbarao. It also implies preserving the value of a currency by ensuring low inflation.

Subbarao's legacy was a troubled one. Aside from a visibly strained relationship with the government, his last days at the RBI were marred by the *Cobra Post* expose that revealed the RBI's lassitude as a supervisory body and how leading Indian banks had been violating KYC (know your customer) guidelines. Subbarao was also drawn into controversy when he forwarded a whistleblowing complaint sent to him in October 2012 by noted activist Devidas Tuljapurkar, detailing a fraud committed in the Bank of Maharashtra. Subbarao forwarded this complaint to the Bank of Maharashtra, the management of which then allegedly harassed Tuljapurkar (a former director of the same bank). It was a dismal failure of the RBI's whistleblowing policy.

Many of Subbarao's decisions were heavily criticized from the beginning. Some of his predecessors in the finance ministry disagreed over his decision to raise interest rates in 2010 and then ease them later. They were also not fans of the way he handled management of monetary policy, relations with the government and the exchange rate. Subbarao was often compared to his predecessor, Y.V. Reddy, who kept his cards close to his chest and surprised markets with his policy measures. Subbarao, in comparison, stood out in his introduction of forward guidance, a practice in vogue in the USA for almost 20 years that saw central banks being transparent about monetary policy. He also focussed on financial inclusion. Thorat, who was deputy governor during Subbarao's tenure, speaks admiringly of his desire to not let the RBI be perceived as an enigma by anybody and of his inclusiveness and encouragement of participation. He was known as a 'consensus man', soft-spoken and ever-smiling, welcoming opinions from all quarters but speaking his own mind. In the five years of Subbarao's tenure, the rupee sank from ₹44 to ₹69 to a dollar. At the time of writing (September 2021), the rupee had depreciated by approximately 1 per cent, going from ₹69 to ₹72 to a dollar. Those who support Subbarao say that while indeed there was a risk of inflation, he could have been mindful of the fact that aggressively tightening rates would have hurt the economy more. Thorat defends him saying that once he realized inflation was anti-growth and anti-poor, he did not hesitate to act. Rangarajan, a mentor to Subbarao and former head of the prime minister's economic advisory council, also empathized with Subbarao and said that the RBI alone could not be held responsible for the rupee when the external sector was under such pressure. There can be no 'walking alone' in times of crisis.

ANECDOTE: PRICE STABILITY—A COMMON MAN'S PERSPECTIVE

The key focus of monetary policy is to assure price stability by controlling money supply or by managing interest rates. Once, sometime after becoming the finance minister of India in the early 1990s, Manmohan Singh was visiting M. Narasimham's home when Mrs Narasimham apparently asked him, 'Manmohan, you say that inflation has come down. But, when I buy vegetables, I still have to pay higher prices than before.' Singh, who had himself been an RBI governor, replied, 'In fact, my wife Gursharan also asks me the same question. And I tell her that I really find it difficult to answer!'[6]

---

[6]Reddy, Y.V., *Advice and Dissent: My Life in Public Service*, Harper Collins, 2018, p. 185.

Both Singh and Narasimham, being past governors, knew it was a very complex procedure to measure inflation, which is an index of change in the general level of prices as distinct from relative prices. A reduction in inflation does not mean that the general level of prices has come down. It only means that the rate of increase of the general level of prices has come down. However, this is very difficult for the masses to understand, as they expect the prices to cool when the inflation index comes down.

Incidentally, even Subbarao faced this question as governor in 2012, and he said, 'As a young man with a lot of hair, I paid about a tenth of what I pay now as a bald or almost-bald man.' While discussing the problems of measuring inflation, he said, 'I struggle to determine how much of that is inflation and how much is the premium I pay the barber for the privilege of cutting the governor's non-existent hair.'[7]

Subbarao describes a chat with his barber in Hyderabad in his memoir:

> The other day, when I was in Hyderabad, I went to my regular barber for a haircut. In the inevitable barber–client conversation, it was our practice to talk about his children, my children, local politics and Bollywood. But this time round he was seeing me for the first time after I became governor. Even as he was preparing to apply scissors to my hair, he asked, 'When are you going to cut interest rates?' I was exasperated by even my barber not giving me any respite from interest rates. Clearly wanting to take my mind off stressful issues, I tried to divert the topic. But he seemed bent on dispensing wisdom and persisted with the banter on interest rates. I got irritated and snapped at him, 'What do you know about interest rates and how does it matter to

[7]'Subbarao's Lesson in Inflation', *Business World*, 8 Novermber 2014, https://bit.ly/3IfpwMJ. Accessed on 20 February 2023.

you at all? Why don't you just leave me alone?' He smiled and said, 'I don't know much about interest rates, but I do know that if I talk about them, your hair will rise and it will be easier to cut it.'[8]

---

[8]Subbarao, Duvvuri, *Who Moved My Interest Rate: Leading the Reserve Bank through Five Turbulent Years*, Penguin, 2016, pp. 124–6.

23

Raghuram Rajan

Dr Raghuram Rajan assumed charge as the twenty-third governor of the RBI on 4 September 2013 and held office until September 2016. He is one of the youngest people to ever hold this position. His style earned him the media nickname of 'Rockstar Rajan'.

Raghuram Govinda Rajan is the son of former intelligence officer R. Govinda Rajan. He was born on 3 February 1963 in Bhopal, Madhya Pradesh. Rajan studied electrical engineering at IIT Delhi, and went on to study at IIMA. He completed his doctorate from the MIT Sloan School of Management, where he wrote his thesis on banking. He has taught at several reputed institutions, including the University of Chicago and MIT Sloan. Rajan has also been the economic counsellor and director of research for the IMF and chief economic advisor to the finance ministry of India. His research interests are banking, corporate finance and economic development. Rajan's pragmatism and foresight earned him commendations for predicting the financial crisis of 2008. Before he was appointed as the governor, Rajan was appointed officer on special duty in the RBI from August 2013 to assist D. Subbarao in fighting currency volatility.

Rajan announced a slew of new measures in his first press conference on 5 September 2013. Banks would have a three-month window until 30 November 2013 to swap their foreign currency non-resident deposits for three years and above at a fixed rate of 3.5 per cent. He also announced significant concessions for banks to raise Tier I capital from external sources. He opened separate window for oil marketing companies for their dollar requirements. He also raised the benchmark interest rate from 7.5 per cent to 7.75 per cent, and again in January 2014 to 8 per cent. By 30 November 2013, India had amassed $34 billion in the Tier I capital scheme. The rupee consequently stabilized at ₹62 to a dollar. After stabilizing the rupee, Rajan shifted his focus to bringing about systemic changes in monetary policy.

Rajan introduced several measures to modernize and liberalize the Indian banking system. He was clear about his intention to defend the value of the rupee, both internally and externally. In *I Do What I Do*, a collection of Rajan's speeches with additional commentary, Rajan writes that his key policy objectives were to present a façade of confidence to assure the public and the investors that the RBI knew what had to be done; to emphasize the RBI's commitment to bringing down inflation; to signal that the RBI could be bold and farsighted when the need arose and finally, to set standards for transparency and predictability.[1]

Rajan also announced in his first speech the setting up of a committee to be chaired by deputy governor Urjit Patel, whose aim would be to examine what needed to be done to revise and strengthen the RBI's monetary policy framework. The committee submitted its report on 21 January 2014, and its recommendations were mostly accepted by the RBI. Accordingly, Rajan announced in a press conference the adoption of a flexible inflation targeting policy framework with a target of 4 per cent stable consumer price inflation rate for the economy over a two-year period. This was opposed to the multiple indicator approach propounded by Bimal Jalan in 1997 and has been in use ever since. Rajan also

[1]Rajan, Raghuram, *I Do What I Do*, Harper Business, 2018, p. 15.

announced the proposed delegation of the monetary policy-making process to a monetary policy committee comprising the governor, a deputy governor handling monetary policy, an executive director from the monetary policy division and two members nominated by the governor of the RBI. This was a key policy decision: Until that time, the governor made the final decision when it came to monetary policy. These decisions were, of course, subject to government approval but it was a significant shift regardless. The government accepted Rajan's proposal for a monetary policy committee, even if it would require amendments to the RBI Act. It did not accept Rajan's suggestions for the composition of the monetary policy committee, seeking to both appoint more independent members to the committee and take away the governor's veto power. This was harshly criticized by the media.

In May 2014, the BJP-led National Democratic Alliance won the general elections and Narendra Modi became the prime minister of India. Speculation abounded as to how the relationship between the Modi government and the Rajan-led RBI would develop. There was much common ground between the two, such as boosting consumption and the use of technology to foster financial inclusion. The government expressed its full support to Rajan in his efforts to tame inflation. In an interview the same year, Rajan said his major targets as governor of the RBI were to lower inflation, increase savings and deepen financial markets. Of these, he believed reducing inflation was the most important, and his dedication bore fruit. He successfully brought down retail inflation to 3.78 per cent in July 2015 from 9.8 per cent in September 2013, making it the lowest it had been since the 1990s. Wholesale inflation was down to a historic low of –4.05 per cent in July 2015 from an earlier 6.1 per cent in September 2013.

Under Rajan, the RBI followed the global norm and adopted consumer price index as the key indicator of inflation despite the government recommending otherwise. India's foreign-exchange reserves grew 30 per cent stronger than they were two years prior to his tenure. His approach to banking services was rather conservative; of the 25 applications received, only two applicants were given approval to set up universal banks—IDFC Bank and Bandhan Bank. In the meantime, the RBI had received the report of the Nachiket Mor Committee in January 2014. The committee, set up to give recommendations on leveraging technology for financial penetration, had recommended setting up payment banks. A payment bank was a relatively new concept envisaging the facilitation of electronic transactions by leveraging Aadhaar infrastructure. In July 2014, the RBI issued draft guidelines for issue of licenses for payment banks and small finance banks. The RBI had also issued guidelines on 1 August 2016 for 'on tap' licensing of universal banks in the private sector. There was a large number of applications from various players for setting up payment banks and small finance banks. At this juncture, the RBI issued licenses to eleven payment banks.

The decision to issue licenses to payment banks and small finance banks was not welcomed by commercial banks. These banks were apprehensive that the new banks, with better technology and lesser administrative cost, would be able to offer better rates to depositors and would result in commercial banks losing deposits. However, Rajan dismissed such fears and explained that these banks were necessary to achieve better financial inclusion. He also hoped that the increasing competition would lead to the government exiting banking and focusing on public welfare.

Rajan had put forth the idea of organizing the central office departments of the RBI into five clusters: regulation and banking services; supervision and risk management; financial markets and infrastructure; monetary stability and operations and human resources. Rajan felt that an additional deputy governor's post was required for monetary policy. He had planned that the fifth deputy governor would act as chief operating officer and would be in charge of licensing. Rajan felt that the move would free the governor and deputy governors from the day-to-day working of the RBI. All the potential contenders he had in mind were past colleagues or outsiders to the RBI. The move was met with vehement resistance within and outside the RBI. Even the UPA government pointed out that amendments to laws would be required to create the post of the fifth deputy governor.

Rajan's tenure saw the Modi government unveil a number of financial inclusion initiatives. In 2014, Prime Minister Modi announced a scheme called the Pradhan Mantri Jan-Dhan Yojana. The scheme was a financial inclusion drive whereby every family without a bank account would be allowed to open one and become part of the formal economy. Modi asked the RBI and banks to devise minimum KYC formalities but maintain the Aadhaar link for insurance benefits. The government expected the scheme to be implemented rapidly and at once, but banks were sceptical as these accounts would have low balances or zero balances. They could not be expected to become borrowers. Banks were also worried about the extra paperwork involved.

Rajan too was somewhat sceptical. He doubted whether such accounts would be used. There was also the danger of opening multiple accounts in a hurry; he advised banks to focus on universal coverage rather than number of accounts opened. In spite of the initial scepticism, the scheme was a roaring success. Within just 45 days, approximately 550 lakh accounts were opened under the scheme. As of January 2021, the total number of accounts opened is around 420 lakh, of which 360 lakh accounts are operational.

Another of Modi's initiatives was 'Make in India'. Its objectives were to increase the growth rate of manufacturing to between 12 and 14 per cent per annum, to increase the share of manufacturing in the GDP to 25 per cent and to create at least a 100 million jobs through manufacturing by 2022. In a lecture in December 2014,

Rajan remarked that the scheme would be more successful if it was 'Make in India, Make for India'. India had a large market and domestic savings—the scheme would be a great success. It would be led by growth and driven by India's own demand. Rajan also speculated on whether the scheme envisaged export-led growth as was the case with China a few decades ago, stressing that times had changed and India needed to follow a unique path. He also voiced his reservations on export subsidies in the same lecture. Rajan was correct in his analysis and his advice to the government was sound, but his remarks were understood as belittling the government's efforts to boost domestic manufacturing. The rift between the government and the RBI began to widen again.[2]

By the second half of 2014, crude oil prices had begun moderating and fallen to $80 from $110. This was a windfall for a country like India, whose prospects for a better balance of payments position had improved. The government announced the deregulation of domestic oil prices and the end of subsidies on petroleum products. The RBI welcomed the move as it would enhance fiscal discipline and also give the RBI a chance to loosen monetary policy and start reducing policy rates. In early 2015, the RBI announced several policy rate cuts since inflation was coming down. The RBI continued to reduce rates but banks would not pass on the rate cuts to customers. This became a point of contention between banks and the RBI. The government was also concerned, because inflation had come down but growth was still not picking up. By mid-2015, the fiscal deficit was in control, inflation had come down and oil prices had moderated. Growth still had not picked up. There was almost no credit offtake. The government had issued a new GDP series and had made changes in the method of calculation. The GDP was now said to be expanding under the new series, but this statement was disconnected from the

[2]Ibid. 168.

ground reality of stagnating growth. The RBI, banks, economists and even government functionaries were baffled. In reality, banks were heavily burdened by NPAs, which was impacting growth. Rajan realized that there was an urgent need to clean the bank balance sheets since bank managements were in no position to lend with stressed balance sheets. He felt that the only way for them to supply the economy's need for credit, which is essential for higher economic growth, was to clean up. Stringent action needed to be taken against delinquent borrowers, and genuinely good borrowers needed to be protected or even incentivized. Therefore, Rajan announced the introduction of marginal cost of funds-based lending to ensure the benefit of rate cuts was speedily passed on to the borrowers.

The RBI then started to focus on the menace of NPAs in the banking system, particularly in the public-sector banks. The problem was not only the borrowers who were defaulters but also the banks that were reluctant to recognize the accounts as NPAs. Rajan asked banks to speed up their recognition of NPA accounts, and flagged the growing number of NPAs as a serious concern and a severe threat to capital adequacy.[3] He initiated a focussed scrutiny of bank balance sheets and advised banks to make more provisions for NPAs, even if it impacted their profitability. He also asked banks to be firm while dealing with borrowers.

Rajan recognized that it was difficult for banks to take action against large corporations even if they were big defaulters, since the leaders of these corporations were cosy with those in power. Consequently, banks had adopted ingenious methods of evergreening the accounts of such corporations. They also feared being pulled up by vigilance authorities for any mistakes they made. This led to the piling up of large unrecognized NPAs that were an immediate threat to the banking system. This was just the

[3]'Raghuram Rajan Warns Bankers on "Ever-Greening" of Bad Loans', *NDTV*, 15 November 2013, https://bit.ly/3YIb4UM. Accessed on 20 February 2023.

tip of the iceberg: Certain customers had multiple identity cards in banks. Incorrect data was uploaded to credit rating agencies, which meant that banks were misled on the customers. Customers could take multiple loans from different banks undetected. There was no end to what needed fixing.

The government and the RBI worked together to end the NPA menace and stem the rot. The government formed the Bank Boards Bureau under former Comptroller and Auditor General Vinod Rai. The aim of the bureau was to review governance practices in banks and recommend improvements. After years of warnings on exuberant lending, the RBI finally launched the asset quality review to force banks to square off their books. In the absence of a functioning bankruptcy code, the RBI put together a number of schemes to facilitate bank resolution of distress and repeatedly re-examined the schemes to see how they could be tweaked to facilitate resolution. Unfortunately, with the exception of a few hard-charging and conscientious bankers, the general mood among the bankers was to continue to extend and pretend. Fearing they would be held accountable for any concession they made, they constantly (and perhaps understandably) avoided making decisions. As the RBI found banks reluctant to recognize the problem, it decided not just to end forbearance but also to force them to clean up their balance sheets. Rajan's tough stance against NPAs won him the International Banker of the Year Award in early 2016.

Rajan's term was to end in September 2016 and, considering his performance, it was widely expected that his term would be extended. However, Rajan was known to speak his mind and would sometimes comment on subjects not related to his job as governor. His remarks were often quoted out of context and sensationalized by journalists. It is possible that the unprecedented level of media attention exacerbated Rajan's tensions with the government.

Subramanian Swamy, a nominated member of the Rajya Sabha, was particularly vicious towards Rajan and consistently demanded his termination. He claimed that Rajan's foreign education meant he was 'mentally not fully Indian' and that Rajan was responsible for destroying Indian industry.[4] Swamy repeatedly alleged that Rajan was unpatriotic and his loyalties lay elsewhere. It was hardly unusual for the governor of the RBI to have tensions with the government. Rajan's predecessor, D. Subbarao, had often clashed with Finance Minister P. Chidambaram. But Rajan drew unusually vicious ire and equally impassioned defence from people who were otherwise uninterested in the RBI. Rajan's commitment to India was defended by ordinary people on social media and movie stars alike. The debate had nothing to do with Rajan's monetary policies or the RBI as an institution,and was instead entirely oriented on Rajan's personality and good looks.

Swamy's allegations would be beneath the dignity of the lowest office, but it was particularly unfortunate to see them being flung at Rajan, who had been sincere in doing his job to the best of his remarkable abilities. There were indications that the government would extend Rajan's term, but Rajan announced that he would retire after his term ended on 4 September 2013 to return to Chicago and resume teaching. Swamy did not stop his tirade against Rajan until Modi intervened and shut down the unbridled criticism of Rajan, who could not reply to the accusations due to the nature of his position as a bureaucrat. Prime Minister Modi was full of praise for Rajan's service and his patriotism, and it sweetened the otherwise bitter end to Rajan's dedicated and successful tenure.[5]

---

[4]'Sack Raghuram Rajan, He's a Disaster…Mentally Not Fully Indian: Subramanian Swamy to PM Modi', *The Indian Express*, 18 May 2016, https://bit.ly/3EnvaLE. Accessed on 20 February 2023.

[5]'Modi Praises Rajan, Disapproves Swamy's Remarks', *Rediff.com*, 27 June 2016, https://bit.ly/3IbRJnH. Accessed on 20 February 2023.

Rajan was balanced in his approach to the governor's relationship with the government. The RBI governor could not be the government's thoughtless cheerleader, nor could he be an unconstrained critic. The eyes on him demand that he picks his battles carefully and how he fights them. Sometimes, however, it meant saying 'no' firmly. It was easy for the governor of the RBI to be seen as a critic by the press and social media as it was an easy and dramatic narrative to spin. But that fear of misinterpretation should not come in the way of discharging one's responsibilities. In Rajan's view, it was important that India steered a stable path when surrounded by so much global risk, and he met with the government regularly to share perspectives and establish mutual understanding. He believed strongly in speaking up when one's responsibilities demanded it, a lesson he tried to impart to his junior colleagues at the RBI as well. Indeed, Rajan was acutely aware of how many young people looked up to him. He was not one for social media, but the relentless press attention made him realize that young people saw the governor of the RBI as a role model to emulate. He had a responsibility, then, to display unparalleled professional integrity over and above the requisite personal integrity.

As the RBI governor, Rajan forged a reputation as an outspoken technocrat who articulated his views as effectively in private as he did in his public speeches. He was regarded as a fine combination of an academic well versed in banking theory and a practising central banker. In an article for *Open*, Siddhartha Singh compared him to Janet Yellen, chair of the US Federal Reserve, and Stanley Fischer, vice-chair of the Fed and former governor of the Bank of Israel.[6]

Rajan believed in the potential of capitalism to effect good in people's lives. Tasked with preparing a report on potential

---

[6]Singh, Siddharth, 'Raghuram Rajan: The Hesitant Memoirist', *Open*, 20 September 2017, http://bit.ly/3Ew7qVZ. Accessed on 31 January 2023.

financial sector reforms by Montek Singh Ahluwalia in 2006, Rajan's report ('A Hundred Small Steps') provided a clear blueprint for the future. The report was excellent, but then-Governor Y.V. Reddy did not buy in, just as he had refused to do with the report on participatory notes. Rajan's report had a simple plan: open up, liberalize, include and let a hundred flowers bloom. He wrote:

> The most important shift in paradigm is to alter the emphasis somewhat from the large-bank-led, public-sector-dominated, mandate-ridden, branch-expansion-focused strategy for inclusion. The poor need efficiency, innovation, and value for money, which can come from motivated financiers who have a low-cost structure and thus see the poor as profitable, but who also have the capacity of making decisions quickly and with minimum paperwork.[7]

Some of Rajan's proposals made sense and were implemented after he became governor. One such proposal was freeing banks to set up branches and ATMs anywhere. Domestic banks have not had the freedom to set up branches anywhere thus far and would not have anticipated such liberalization (which was not an element of the RBI roadmap). His approach to policy was grounded in pragmatism as much as in theory. Speaking at a conference in New Delhi, Rajan suggested that global monetary policy decisions be subjected to traffic lights known as Rajan's 'traffic signal rules'. The speech pitched a rule-based global monetary policy system. The traffic light rule was intuitive:

> If a certain monetary policy has positive effects on both the home country and the foreign country, it should be rated green or given a green signal. The policies that get the orange light come attached with a 'tread with caution'

[7]Planning Commission, Government of India, *A Hundred Small Steps: Report of the Committee on Financial Sector Reforms*, SAGE Publications, 2009, p. 7.

> tag. Not unlike on the roads. Then there are the policies that get a red signal. 'Stop or else.' [8]

Rajan has also published numerous articles in finance and economics journals including the *American Economic Review*, *Journal of Political Economy* and *Oxford Review of Economic Policy*. Rajan has won many awards. According to Clarivate Analytics, a company that does academic and scientific research and maintains a list of dozens of potential Nobel winners based on research citations, Rajan was also a possible nominee. Rajan's name was one of the six economists on the list of probable winners made by the firm, listed along with economists Michael C. Jenson and Stewart C. Myers for their contributions in 'illuminating the dimensions of decisions in corporate finance'.[9] If Rajan had won, he would have become only the second Indian after Amartya Sen in 1998 to ever win a Nobel Prize in economics. He may still make history here as he is one of the sharpest and most rightfully praised minds in economics.

---

[8]Dugal, Ira, 'Raghuram Rajan's Traffic Signal Rules for Global Monetary Policy', *The Mint*, 18 March 2016, http://bit.ly/3m29Aq1. Accessed on 20 January 2023.
[9]'Raghuram Rajan's Name in Clarivate List of Nobel Prize Worthies', *The Economic Times*, 7 October 2017, https://bit.ly/3kbG6W2. Accessed on 20 February 2023.

24

Urjit Patel

Dr Urjit R. Patel assumed charge as the twenty-fourth governor of the RBI in September 2016 after serving as the deputy governor since January 2013. He is an eminent banker, economist and consultant.

Patel was born in Nairobi to a Gujarati family. He completed his doctorate in economics from Yale University, USA, after studying at University of Oxford, UK, and University of London, UK. As the deputy governor of the RBI, Patel chaired the expert committee to revise and strengthen the monetary policy framework. He represented India at BRICS and served at the IMF. Patel was on deputation from the IMF to the RBI from 1996 to 1997, providing advice on development of the debt market, banking sector reforms, pension fund reforms and the evolution of the foreign-exchange market. Patel has worked closely with several central and state government high-level committees, including the task force on direct taxes (the Kelkar Committee) and the committee on civil aviation reforms. He was appointed chairman of the National Institute of Public Finance and Policy (NIPFP) in 2020.

Patel's three-year term as the deputy governor of the RBI had just been extended by another two years in January 2016 when Raghuram Rajan announced his intent to retire from the RBI at the end of his term in September. Patel's appointment was declared by the government in August 2016 and he took charge as the governor in September 2016. After Rajan's stormy tenure, it is likely the government wanted a governor that continued Rajan's policies but was given to fewer words, like Patel.

Patel's biggest challenge was demonetization. On 8 November 2016, Prime Minister Modi suddenly announced the demonetization of the 500- and 1,000-rupee notes with immediate effect, asking citizens to deposit these notes in their possession on or before 30 December 2016. This measure was purportedly implemented to fight black money and the menace of fake currency notes in circulation. In one fell swoop, it demonetized almost 86 per cent of the currency in circulation. The RBI was not party to the decision to demonetize these notes, which was taken at the highest level of India's political leadership.

Raghuram Rajan has mentioned in an interview that there had been some informal discussion on demonetization a few months before the actual announcement was made. He also mentioned that he had advised against it because he felt that the disadvantages of demonetization in the short term far outweighed the advantages in the long run. It is unclear whether the RBI knew before the decision of demonetization was actually taken. What is clear is that a meeting of the RBI's Central Board of Directors was hurriedly called just five hours before the Prime Minister's announcement on 8 November 2016. In the meeting, chaired by Patel, the board endorsed the proposal to withdraw the legal tender status of the 500- and 1,000-rupee notes in circulation. An RTI query revealed that this resolution was actually signed by the governor on 15 December 2016, despite appearing to be passed on five weeks prior.[1] Replying to a query in the Rajya Sabha on 6 February 2017, then-Finance Minister Arun Jaitley

[1]'PM Modi Went Ahead with Demonetisation before RBI's Formal Approval: RTI', *The Indian Express*, 11 March 2019, http://bit.ly/3ILlZra. Accessed on 31 January 2023.

asserted that the RBI board met and recommended of its own volition that the notes be demonetized.[2]

This book cannot explore why demonetization was announced, whether it was the right decision or whether it achieved what it set out to achieve. Previous exercises in demonetization by the British government in 1946 and the Morarji Desai government in 1978 found that almost 95 per cent of the demonetized currency in circulation was deposited in banks, defeating the purpose of demonetization. The year 2016 was no different. As much as 99 per cent of the demonetized currency was deposited in banks. The minutes of the meeting in November showed that the finance ministry had drawn up the proposed demonetization scheme, contending that there was a substantial growth of 500- and 1,000-rupee notes in circulation that was disproportionate to the growth of the economy. The Central Board of the RBI, it is revealed, had disputed the finance ministry's contentions. Most black money is held not in cash but in assets like real estate and gold. Demonetization would likely fail and its impact on India's GDP could be as high as 2 per cent.[3]

The RBI is the sole note-issuing authority and currency manager of the country. It was taking flak for an operation for which it was entirely unprepared, as it was managed by the finance ministry. There were long queues at bank branches. The government had announced that new notes of ₹500, ₹1,000 and ₹2,000 would be issued but done nothing to ensure their availability. ATMs were not equipped to dispense the new notes, which were smaller in size. The RBI staff was restless and uncomfortable with the people deputed from the finance

---

[2]'Consultations on Note Ban Were on Since Feb Last Year: Arun Jaitley', *Business Today*, 7 February 2017, https://bit.ly/3ID7xS4. Accessed on 20 February 2023.

[3]'Demonetisation: RBI Board Disagreed, but Put Its Stamp on the Decision 38 Days Later, Reveals RTI', *Moneylife*, 11 March 2019, https://bit.ly/3kc4WFb. Accessed on 20 February 2023.

ministry to handle the situation. The RBI faced stinging criticism in the media, where it was alleged that the RBI leadership had surrendered before the government and compromised its own autonomy. Patel, not one for many words, did not communicate with the press for almost two weeks after demonetization except in the joint press briefing immediately after it was announced (where he neither endorsed nor distanced himself from the government's decision). Shaktikanta Das, the economic affairs secretary, handled communication through the crisis. Rumours began to spread about Patel, who had worked with the government before taking charge of the RBI and had known Prime Minister Modi since he was the chief minister of Gujarat. Patel had also worked with Reliance Industries in the early years of his career. The media ran with the narrative that Patel was a yes man who worked for the government more than the RBI. It would later be seen that Patel would have had an easier time than he actually did had he been a yes man.

In a monetary policy meeting in January 2014, Rajan had announced raising the key interest rate by 0.25 percentage points but had indicated that no further increase would be required if consumer price inflation stayed on its projected trajectory. In the press briefing that followed the meeting, a reporter asked Rajan why the RBI had acted like a hawk and spoken like a dove. Rajan replied that the RBI was neither a hawk nor a dove but an owl. He asked the then-deputy governor Urjit Patel to elaborate to the audience what he meant. Patel explained that owls were traditionally symbols of wisdom, so the RBI was neither hawk nor dove but an owl that was vigilant when others were resting.[4]

And vigilant he was. During Rajan's tenure, Patel was chairman of the committee appointed to examine what needed to be done

---

[4]'We Are Neither Hawks, nor Doves, We Are Owls: RBI', *Hindustan Times*, 29 January 2014, https://bit.ly/3XKYoec. Accessed on 20 February 2023.

to revise and strengthen the RBI's monetary policy framework. After exhaustive work, the committee submitted its report on 21 January 2014 recommending that targeting inflation be the main focus of monetary policy. It recommended the adoption of a flexible inflation targeting policy framework with approximately 4 per cent as the stable consumer price inflation rate for the economy. It also recommended transferring the RBI's decision-making process to a monetary policy committee comprised of the governor, a deputy governor, an executive director and two members nominated by the governor. Finally, it recommended revamping the RBI's liquidity management as well as the adoption of new policy instruments. These were far-reaching recommendations that were accepted by the governor in toto and by the government with some modifications. The policies framed, based on the recommendations, are being followed consistently.

Another challenge Patel faced was the number of rising NPAs in the banking system, particularly in public-sector banks. In 2014, gross NPAs stood at 3.8 per cent, but rose every year to stand at 10.5 per cent in 2018. Patel introduced the prompt corrective action (PCA) framework for banks that had overshot their gross and net NPA beyond the limit prescribed in RBI directives and where the capital adequacy ratio had fallen below 9 per cent. The RBI put eleven public-sector banks and the IDBI Bank under the PCA framework, imposing restrictions on their operations so as to nurse them back to health.

Patel remained firm on the resolution of bad debts in Indian banks, taking action against powerful business houses if necessary. Sensing that banks were evergreening advances to large corporations under the garb of restructuring, he withdrew all the circulars under which such restructuring was made possible, such as the corporate debt restructuring (CDR) scheme. The RBI made it clear to banks that any debt in default beyond 90 days must be recognized as non-performing and provided for, with recovery proceedings initiated against such borrowers. The government wanted the RBI to be lenient towards these banks because of debts due from power-sector companies, and the RBI's strict action led to a clash between the two. The RBI, having earlier communicated its unwillingness to compromise on the 12 February 2018 circular on defaulting loans, refused to send a representative to a meeting of the Cabinet committee on power-sector loans.

Patel warned private-sector banks that any misgovernance in the identification of NPAs would not be tolerated. He made large banks like Axis Bank and ICICI Bank declare their hidden NPAs and did not hesitate to take action against their chief executive officers (CEOs), who had been in the saddle for years together and did not comply with the RBI's prescriptions in this regard. He also insisted on the government giving the RBI more powers over public-sector banks and criticized the government over the widening fiscal deficit and rising supply of bonds. Patel was of the firm opinion that the public-sector banks were governed by the finance ministry in addition to the RBI, and that this dual power structure was leading to deep fissures in the banking landscape.

Patel visibly strove to protect the RBI's autonomy and authority and faced internal and external challenges to this end. The IMF's 2018 Financial Sector Assessment Program report came as a rude shock to Patel, as it found that the RBI was 'materially non-compliant' in the matter of autonomy.[5] According to the report, while the RBI had budgetary autonomy and adequate resources, it had never had full discretion to take supervisory actions. The report also mentioned that the RBI Act contains a number of powers enabling the central government to supersede the RBI's decisions, which have never been used but whose breadth and very existence undermines the RBI's legal independence. Called before the parliamentary Standing Committee on Finance

---

[5]Patel, Urjit R., *Overdraft: Saving the Indian Saver*, Harper Business, 2020, pp. 73–7.

in 2018, Patel stressed that the RBI's autonomy was key to its functioning. It was essential to maintain the important objective of depositors' interests. An autonomous RBI should also have exclusive control over the country's monetary policy, with only experts and technocrats having a say. Finally, Patel asserted that a high level of central bank reserves is essential to maintain the country's AAA rating.

Dr Manmohan Singh, himself once the governor of the RBI and later finance minister, remarked that the relationship between the RBI and the government was like that of husband and wife, and the differences must be resolved 'in a manner that the two institutions work in harmony'.[6] However, reportedly, the gap between the government and the RBI grew wider. There were disputes on the quantum of profit to be transferred by the RBI to the government. The government also wanted to transfer some of the RBI's reserves. Therefore, Patel appointed the Expert Committee on Economic Capital Framework in November 2018 under the chairmanship of Bimal Jalan, a former governor of the RBI. There was friction regarding the PCA framework that the RBI had imposed on 11 public-sector banks; the government was uncomfortable and wanted it lifted while the RBI refused to toe the government line. There were disputes over the government's suggestion to set up a payments regulator outside the purview of the RBI, to which the RBI publicly objected. There were other confrontations: in light of the Nirav Modi scam detected in the PNB, the government had been critical of the RBI for its laxity in regulation. The government disagreed with Patel's stance on adopting accounting standards based on the International Financial Reporting Standards and stiff Basel-III norms. The government did not want to push for these as these provisions

---

[6] '"Government, RBI Relation Like That of Husband and Wife": Manmohan Singh', *NDTV*, 18 December 2018, https://bit.ly/41aupPV. Accessed on 20 February 2023.

would require banks to maintain more capital. Tensions were soaring. Finally, on 10 October 2018, the government invoked a hitherto unused Section 7 of the RBI Act to enforce the decisions it wanted the RBI to take, and Patel announced his resignation the same day. Although he claimed to be resigning on personal grounds ahead of the end of his term in September 2019, it is likely he wanted to leave with no loss of dignity to either himself or the institution he led.

Patel's resignation came days before the RBI's Central Board met on 14 December. Patel maintained that personal reasons were behind his exit, but many at the RBI believed that his confrontation with the government and its nominees had reached the point of no return. On Patel's resignation, Prime Minister Modi tweeted, 'Dr Urjit Patel is an economist of a very high calibre with a deep and insightful understanding of macro-economic issues. He steered the banking system from chaos to order and ensured discipline. Under his leadership, the RBI brought financial stability.'[7] He further said, 'Dr Urjit Patel is a thorough professional with impeccable integrity. He has been in the Reserve Bank of India for about six years as the deputy governor and governor. He leaves behind a great legacy. We will miss him immensely.'[8]

In his book *Overdraft: Saving the Indian Saver*, Patel strongly criticized the UPA government for the enormous crisis of NPAs in public-sector banks, stating that the UPA failed to create risk controls or ensure adequate management. He noted this as a perennial shortcoming on account of bureaucratic inertia and political meddling. He also questioned the RBI's failure in identifying bad loans before 2014, arguing that the RBI should have put in place stringent checks like stress tests and sensitivity

---

[7]@narendramodi, Twitter, 10 December 2018, 5.55 p.m., https://t.co/DyZUxKIXPv. Accessed on 22 February 2023.

[8]@narendramodi, Twitter, 10 December 2018, 5.56 p.m., https://t.co/NLta1tMLPg. Accessed on 22 February 2023.

analyses. Patel writes that had the Central Bank identified the build-up of risks, it could have tightened lending norms by, for instance, increasing risk weights allotted to various sectors. In his book, Patel writes about the '9R' strategy, which would have saved public savings, rescued the banks and protected them from unscrupulous racketeers. Patel also has several publications in the areas of Indian macroeconomics, monetary policy, public finance, Indian financial sector, international trade and regulatory economics.

TRIVIA

1. The RBI Act does not contain any qualifications for the post of governor. By convention, however, all the governors appointed have been either seasoned bureaucrats with distinguished service records or economists of repute. The governor of the Bank is the chairman of the Central Board of Directors. He enjoys full powers of superintendence and direction of all the affairs and business of the Bank. More importantly, he enjoys a privileged position in the financial system. Although the governor has not been accorded any place of significance in the official warrant of precedence, he is given a very high place in official functions.
2. Under the CAS, advances of ₹1 crore and more would be approved by the governor of the RBI only after they were sanctioned by the boards of the respective banks. A couple of piquant issues came to the fore when some banks sought the RBI's clearance for advance proposals even before they were placed before their own boards of directors. Consequently in November 1968, it was conveyed to banks that the RBI's clearance should be sought only after the advance proposals had been approved by their own boards of directors.
3. The London branch of the Central Bank of India was opened

in the early 1950s and was under the care of Sir Cecil R. Trevor, who had been deputy governor of the RBI until 1949 and was the designated London advisor. He retired in 1967, when Sami J. Patel was appointed manager of the branch. Patel enjoyed the confidence of Trevor and had an excellent rapport with him, enabling him to maintain a high profile. An accommodation bills fraud involving £18,55,400 was detected in April 1970 in the branch, the magnitude of which created ripples in the banking industry. The fraud became the subject of active debate in the Lok Sabha, Rajya Sabha and the media. The role of the head office of the Central Bank of India as well as that of the RBI in supervising foreign branches of Indian banks came under scathing criticism. In fact, the last RBI inspection of the affairs of the Central Bank had taken place in 1968, with the report being finalized in May 1970. It had referred, for the first time, to the irregularities in the accounts of Montex, C. Raman and the Trevor group of accounts. This was the only time a past or present senior functionary of the RBI was found involved in any unsavoury practices, as in this case.

25

Shaktikanta Das

Shaktikanta Das is the twenty-fifth and current governor of the RBI. He is a retired IAS officer of the Tamil Nadu cadre, although he is originally from Odisha.

Das studied history at St. Stephen's College at the University of Delhi. He has served in various positions for both the Government of India, such as economic affairs secretary, revenue secretary, fertilizers secretary, special secretary to the Department of Economic Affairs of the Ministry of Finance and as a joint secretary to the Department of Expenditure of the Ministry of Finance, and the Government of Tamil Nadu, such as principal secretary (Industries), special commissioner (Revenue) and as the district magistrate and collector of Dindigul and Kancheepuram districts in the Tamil Nadu government. He has also served as India's alternate governor for the World Bank, Asian Development Bank, New Development Bank and Asian Infrastructure Investment Bank. He has represented India at the IMF, G20, BRICS and the South Asian Association for Regional Cooperation (SAARC) meets. After his retirement from the IAS on 28 May 2017, Das was appointed a member of the Fifteenth Finance Commission. In December 2018, Das resigned from his position in the Fifteenth Finance Commission to assume the charge of the twenty-fifth governor of the RBI.

Das was appointed as the governor of the RBI on

11 December 2018 for a period of three years. He succeeded Urjit Patel, who had resigned on personal grounds, although it was widely speculated that his resignation was due to the rift created between the RBI and the government over the RBI placing 11 public-sector banks under a PCA framework on account of their enormous stressed assets. After the stormy tenures of Rajan and Patel, the government opted for a career bureaucrat instead of a career economist, as was widely expected. Das, along with Patel, had ably guided India through the demonetization exercise in 2016–17 and had strongly defended the measure in various fora. There was considerable media speculation as to how he would fare as the governor without a formal education in economics and, to his credit, Das has proved many of his critics wrong since 2018.[1]

Das has been outspoken about the lack of governance in banking and has called for tighter rules for state-owned banks, which comprise 60 per cent of India's banking sector. To make the banking system more robust, the RBI is to set up a college for supervisors with the aim of improving supervisory skills. Das has brought in measures to tighten the rules around shadow banking, refusing to bail out non-banking financial companies (NBFCs). He is aiming instead for issues to be managed within the financial system, which is possibly a risky move but one that will reduce dependence on the RBI.[2]

With Das assuming charge of the RBI, lenders outside the traditional bank network have been placed under a greater level of scrutiny. Even housing finance companies have been brought under the regulation of the RBI and will have to adhere to the same framework of rules as that of NBFCs. The RBI is also proactively

---

[1]'Expert Views: India Appoints Shaktikanta Das as RBI Governor', *Reuters*, 11 December 2018, http://bit.ly/3IrjLM2. Accessed on 20 February 2023.

[2]'RBI Governor Shaktikanta Das Named "Central Banker of The Year 2020, Asia-Pacific" by The Banker', *CNBC TV18*, 3 February 2020, https://bit.ly/3KhQWo0. Accessed on 20 February 2023.

providing assistance to India's smaller banks. As the threat from newer micro-finance institutions looms, Das has moved to help the country's urban cooperative banks install a robust IT system that will allow them to offer better banking services at a lower cost and also protect client's money and data.

The RBI, under Das, has also mandated banks to offer benchmark-linked lending rates, with most choosing to follow the RBI's 5.15 per cent repo rate. Das was quoted as saying: 'An environment of macroeconomic stability, as reflected in low and stable inflation, notwithstanding its recent spike that is expected to be transient; a sustainable current account deficit; and rising foreign exchange reserves have contributed towards maintaining financial stability and laying a platform for sustained growth.'[3]

Das' lack of formal education in economics has proven to be a gift that allows him to make unconventional choices with great success. Early in his tenure as governor, in March 2019, Das introduced a $5 billion swap window to infuse durable liquidity in the system. The response from the market participants for the scheme was huge when they offered more than three times the notified amount, which encouraged the central bank to repeat the scheme. He also introduced innovative measures to address issues of liquidity and bond yields. Exploring 'Operation Twist' (a monetary policy intervention by the central bank, conducted through OMOs where the central bank buys long-term government bonds and, at the same time, sells short-term government securities with a view to soften long-term yields and improve monetary transmission) and targeting long-term repo operations to enhance liquidity underlines the governor's penchant for unconventional measures to address critical issues. This has been vital in the COVID-19 pandemic.

---

[3]'RBI Governor Shaktikanta Das Bags "Central Banker of the Year 2020, Asia-Pacific" Award', *Hindu Businessline*, 4 February 2020, http://bit.ly/3lW6m77. Accessed on 24 February 2023.

The RBI also adopted a different approach under Das to address the crisis in Yes Bank and Lakshmi Vilas Bank. In case of the latter, for the first time, an Indian bank was allowed to merge with a foreign lender—DBS Bank India Ltd, the Indian subsidiary of Singapore's DBS Bank. And instead of merging Yes Bank with another lender, the RBI opted for a bank-led rescue scheme, in which several lenders picked up a stake, the government-owned SBI taking a lead by picking up 49 per cent. The HDFC Bank, ICICI Bank, Axis Bank, Kotak Mahindra Bank, etc., also chipped in picking up stakes. This was in contrast to earlier rescue plans when a stronger bank was asked to absorb a failing one, for instance, the Global Trust Bank being asked to merge with the OBC.

Das's ability to surprise markets continuously has not gone unnoticed by central bank watchers. He recognized the economic slowdown early and started to reduce interest rates from February 2019. Now in the fourth year of his tenure, all eyes are on whether he allows business barons to open banks. An internal working group of the RBI has recommended granting banking licence to industrial houses that invited sharp reactions from different quarters with former RBI Governor Raghuram Rajan and Deputy Governor Viral Acharya terming the move as a 'bad idea'. Das, however, tried to distance himself from the recommendations of the report as he said, '[L]et me say very clearly that it is a report by an internal working group of the RBI. It should not be seen as RBI's point of view or decision. That has to be very clearly understood.'[4] Das's decision on opening up or not the banking sector to corporations could define his term as the governor of the RBI.

Another important issue is the setting up of a bad bank to take over NPAs in the banking system. The idea of setting

---

[4]'Edited Transcript of Reserve Bank of India's Monetary Policy Press Conference', *Reserve Bank of India*, https://bit.ly/3kipyf8. Accessed on 1 February 2023.

up a bad bank to help the banking system of the country had picked up after Economic Affairs Secretary Tarun Bajaj said in December 2020 that the government was exploring all options, including a bad bank, to improve the health of the lenders in the country. Das said that the idea of a bad bank has been under discussion for a long time but added that the RBI tries to keep its regulatory framework in sync with the requirement of the times. 'We are open (to looking at a bad bank proposal) in the sense, if any proposal comes, we will be examining it and issuing the regulatory guidelines. But then it is for the government and the private players to plan for it,' Das said.[5] He added that the RBI would only take a view on any proposal only after examining it. The proposed bad bank, considered crucial in helping extract capital stuck in soured loans, will be a new asset reconstruction company set up by public-sector lenders to take over bad assets. Following the announcement in the 2021–22 Budget to set up the first-ever bad bank in India, India Debt Resolution Company Ltd, an asset management company, has been set up, which will work in tandem with the National Asset Reconstruction Company Ltd to streamline and square off bad loans.

Another major move during Das's time has been the merger of banks: Eight nationalized banks were merged with other banks in 2019 in a phased manner. Allahabad Bank was merged with the Indian Bank, OBC and United Bank of India (UBI) were merged with the PNB, Vijaya Bank and Dena Bank were merged with Bank of Baroda, Syndicate Bank was merged with Canara Bank and Andhra Bank and Corporation Bank were merged with Union Bank. Except for a few hiccups, the process was largely successful.

The RBI has also encouraged the use of the latest technology in making Indian banking seamless and easy. Areas of blockchain

[5]'RBI Open to Bad Bank Proposal: Shaktikanta Das.' *The Indian Express*, 17 January 2021, http://bit.ly/3xJXrsn. Accessed on 31 January 2023.

technology are also being looked into for their feasibility and possible applicability in India, although the RBI has told the government that it is not in favour of introduction of cryptocurrency in India.

One of the major disputes between the RBI and the government during Urjit Patel's regime was about the surplus distribution policy or how much dividend should be paid by the RBI to the government. There was no accepted policy on this issue. Under the chairmanship of Bimal Jalan, in November 2018, Patel had appointed the Expert Committee on Economic Capital Framework. The Bimal Jalan Committee aimed to review the current economic capital framework. The economic capital framework provides a methodology for determining the appropriate level of risk provisions and profit distribution to be made under Section 47 of the RBI Act, 1934. The committee submitted its report in August 2019, basing its recommendations on the consideration of the role of central banks' financial resilience, cross-country practices, statutory provisions and the impact of the RBI's public-policy mandate and operating environment on its balance sheet and the risks involved. The RBI accepted the recommendations in toto and transferred ₹176,000 crore in 2020 and ₹99,122 crore in 2021 to the central government as dividend and excess capital.

Perhaps the most daunting challenge Das has faced is the COVID-19 pandemic. The RBI was prompt in addressing the economic stress arising due to the nationwide lockdown the government was forced to announce in March 2020. The RBI responded with a 115-basis point rate cut between March and May 2020. Despite inflation staying above the tolerance band of 6 per cent for seven months, the RBI made its stance clear that revival of economic growth on a durable basis and mitigating the impact of the pandemic on the economy were its top priorities.

COVID-19 has strained the resources of all countries and left many of them economically battered. Tasked with maintaining economic stability in an endless crisis, the role of the RBI has become even more crucial than it was before. Das has shown strength and resolve to keep the Indian economy as unaffected by the pandemic as possible with sound and timely reforms. A few key things he announced in this regard are reduction in interest rates, temporary changes in NPA norms and allowance of one-time restructuring of viable and standard MSME loans. During the second wave of the pandemic in April–May 2021, he made available to banks an additional liquidity support of ₹50,000 crore. The battle against COVID-19 was handled remarkably well. It is good to see that Das is handling the situation reasonably well on various fronts, including the institute's autonomy, the kind of reforms being brought in and the RBI's rapport with the government, critics, press and social media.

It may be recalled that when Patel resigned and Das took over as the governor, India's foreign-exchange reserves were at $393 billion. They crossed the $638 billion mark as of September 2021. Thus, there was an accretion of about $245 billion to the forex kitty. The unprecedented liquidity released in the system by world governments (particularly the US government) since March 2020 as part of COVID-19 relief packages had led stock markets across the globe to unprecedented bullishness. India was no exception. The major flow of dollars was in the form of portfolio investment. Despite so much liquidity gushing into the system, not only had the rupee remained comparatively stable but even inflation had remained under control.

Since early 2020, particularly after the amendment in Banking Regulation Act, 1949, Das has taken many steps to reform and strengthen the cooperative banking sector. These include the implementation of governance-strengthening measures like the compulsory appointment of a board of management with more than 50 per cent of the members being experts in fields of accounting, finance, law and so on; the approval of managing director (MD) or CEO appointments from the RBI; requiring MDs and CEOs of cooperative banks to have certain basic qualifications and so on. The cooperative banking sector is politically sensitive and not many governors have bothered to touch it in the past. Das has proved to be an exception. An expert committee on urban cooperative banks was set up in February 2021 under the chairmanship of former deputy governor of the RBI, N.S. Vishwanathan. The expert committee submitted its report on 23 August 2021 in two parts. The recommendations of the committee have been accepted by the RBI with some modifications.

Another important feature of Das's tenure is a spate of penalties levied on all types of banks and NBFCs for violation of guidelines of the RBI, particularly those connected to the classification of advances, provisioning and loans to directors. None of the banks or NBFCs have been spared, be they public-sector banks, private-sector banks, cooperative banks or district central banks. The underlying message is clear: The RBI guidelines cannot be taken lightly and any violation of these guidelines will not be tolerated, big or small.

Das's appointment as the RBI governor received generally positive responses, and unlike many governors before him, he has been able to maintain a positive rapport with the finance minister. Das worked under Arun Jaitley when the latter was the finance minister from 2014 to 2019 and Das was the economic affairs secretary. It was easier for him to maintain coordination with the finance ministry as Jaitley was still the finance minister. However, Jaitley resigned from the Union Cabinet due to ill health in May 2019 and Nirmala Sitharaman took over as the finance minister. Das has been able to maintain excellent coordination and cooperation with her, too, and the full support of the finance ministry has likely helped his pursuit of banking sector reforms.

TRIVIA

1. Fourteen major commercial banks were nationalized in 1969 when L.K. Jha was the governor of the RBI, while six private-sector banks were nationalized in 1980 when I.G. Patel was the governor. However, the nationalization of banks in 1969 was at the insistence of the government while the nationalization in 1980 was at the insistence of the RBI.
2. The consolidation of the banking sector started during the tenure of Y.V. Reddy when the State Bank of Saurashtra was merged with the SBI in 2008. The State Bank of Indore was merged with the SBI in 2010 during D. Subbarao's tenure. It was in Urjit Patel's term that BMB and five associate banks of SBI merged with SBI in 2017. These banks were the SBBJ, SBM, SBT, SBH and SBP.
3. The consolidation of the banking sector gained momentum during the tenure of Shaktikanta Das when Dena Bank and Vijaya Bank were merged with the Bank of Baroda in 2019. The process was further strengthened in 2020 when OBC and UBI were merged with PNB; Syndicate Bank was merged with Canara Bank; Corporation Bank and Andhra Bank were merged with Union Bank of India and Allahabad Bank was merged with Indian Bank. There are now only 12 public-sector banks remaining as of 1 April 2021.
4. It is widely speculated in banking circles that another milestone likely to be reached during the tenure of Shaktikanta Das is the privatization of the IDBI Bank, Bank of Maharashtra, Indian Overseas Bank, UCO Bank, Punjab & Sind Bank and Central Bank of India.

List of RBI Governors and Their Tenures

Sr. No.	Name of the Governor	Period of Service	Term	State
1	Sir Osborne Smith	01/04/1935 to 30/06/1937	27 Months	Australia
2	Sir James Taylor	01/07/1937 to 17/02/1943	5 Years, 7 Months, 17 Days	Great Britain
3	Sir C.D. Deshmukh	11/08/1943 to 30/06/1949	5 Years, 10 Months, 20 Days	Maharashtra
4	Sir Benegal Rama Rau	01/07/1949 to 14/01/1957	7 Years, 6 Months, 14 Days	Karnataka
5	K.G. Ambegaokar	14/01/1957 to 28/02/1957	46 Days	Maharashtra
6	H.V.R. Iengar	01/03/1957 to 28/02/1962	5 Years	Tamil Nadu
7	P.C. Bhattacharyya	01/03/1962 to 30/06/1967	5 Years, 4 Months	West Bengal
8	Laxmi Kant Jha	01/07/1967 to 03/05/1970	2 Years, 10 Months, 3 Days	Bihar
9	B.N. Adarkar	04/05/1970 to 15/06/1970	43 Days	Maharashtra
10	S. Jagannathan	16/06/1970 to 19/05/1975	4 Years, 11 Months, 3 Days	Tamil Nadu

11	N.C. Sengupta	19/05/1975 to 19/08/1975	3 Months	West Bengal
12	K.R. Puri	20/08/1975 to 02/05/1977	1 Year, 8 Months, 12 Days	Punjab
13	M. Narasimham	02/05/1977 to 30/11/1977	6 Months, 28 Days	Andhra Pradesh
14	Dr I.G. Patel	01/12/1977 to 15/09/1982	4 Years, 9 Months, 15 Days	Gujarat
15	Dr Manmohan Singh	16/09/1982 to 14/01/1985	2 Years, 3 Months, 28 Days	Punjab
16	Amitav Ghosh	15/01/1985 to 04/02/1985	21 Days	West Bengal
17	R.N. Malhotra	04/02/1985 to 22/12/1990	5 Years, 10 Months, 18 Days	Punjab
18	S. Venkataramanan	22/12/1990 to 21/12/1992	2 Years	Tamil Nadu
19	Dr C. Rangarajan	22/12/1992 to 21/11/1997	4 Years 11 Months	Tamil Nadu
20	Dr Bimal Jalan	22/11/1997 to 06/09/2003	5 Years. 9 Months, 14 Days	Rajasthan
21	Dr Y.V. Reddy	06/09/2003 to 05/09/2008	5 Years	Andhra Pradesh
22	Dr D. Subbarao	05/09/2008 to 04/09/2013	5 Years	Andhra Pradesh
23	Dr Raghuram Rajan	04/09/ 2013 to 04/09/2016	2 Years, 6 Months	Madhya Pradesh
24	Dr Urjit Patel	05/09/2016 to 10/12/2018	2 Years, 3 Months	Gujarat
25	Shaktikanta Das	13/12/2018 to present	4 years, 1 Month+	Odisha

Acknowledgements

This book has been made possible by many people, and it is only fair that I acknowledge their help with an appropriate mention. The first in a long line of persons I am indebted to is R.L. Sahoo, the chief archivist at the RBI Archives, located in the College of Agricultural Banking Campus in Pune, whom I first met in 2017. It was he who led me to Bakhtiar Dadabhoy, the author of the critically acclaimed *Barons of Banking: Glimpses of Indian Banking History*. Sahoo told me that archival material for the book had been supplied by the RBI Archives. I immediately purchased the book and attempted to ascertain the whereabouts of its author. After a few hits and misses, I discovered, to my pleasant surprise, that Dadabhoy was a resident of Pune at the time. I wasted no time in contacting him and he agreed to meet me immediately.

It was the start of a friendship that lasts to this day. Dadabhoy has been warm and encouraging and gave me his views on the contents of the proposed book. He has been a mentor to me throughout this project, and his enthusiasm for the book rivals mine. Dadabhoy has been a constant source of guidance and encouragement and has read successive drafts of the book. He has proved to be an excellent sounding board and has been invaluable in offering useful perspectives and making insightful suggestions. He has also served as a diligent editor, and his efforts have added clarity and polish to many rough edges. His many suggestions have greatly improved the final product. I cannot thank him enough for his assistance, given unstintingly and with such good cheer.

I am also obliged to Subir Das, a senior banker, who not only encouraged me but kept prodding me to finish what I had started during periods when enthusiasm and energy appeared to flag. He too has read successive drafts and, with his insightful suggestions, gave me the benefit of his four-decade-long career in banking. His observations have been invaluable in improving the usefulness of the book. Bajrangdas Lohiya, an entrepreneur and winner of many industrial excellence awards, has been a guru and mentor to me for the last three decades. His sage counsel, suggestions and encouragement have been of great help. I would like to thank both Subir Das and Bajrangdas Lohiya.

CA Shreeya Dandi has assisted me in this project throughout, and CA Bhagyashree Kankaria, my partner, handled the routine work with aplomb, leaving me time to work on the book. Aradhana Dwivedi-Verma took up the editing of the book and did a splendid job. I convey my sincere thanks to all three of them. My thanks are also due to Rupa Publications and the team, particularly Rudra Narayan Sharma and Smita Mathur, for their invaluable support. In endeavors such as these, where solitude is a prerequisite, it is the family that makes sacrifices. All the time I have spent on the book was rightfully theirs and so grateful thanks are also owed to my wife Manju and daughter Tanvi, who shared their lives with those of 25 RBI governors over the last few years. I only hope that this book justifies this neglect.

Usha Thorat, Meena Hemchandra and P.P. Ramachandran were forthcoming with their comments and advice. I express my gratitude to them for investing their time and energy in this book. Similar thanks go out to Honourable Union Minister Nitin Gadkari for writing the Foreword. Last but not the least, I would like to thank Dr C. Rangarajan, a former governor himself, for his comments and for agreeing to write the Foreword to the book. It is to him that this book is dedicated. I can only hope that this book meets his high standards.

Index